Survey Responses From the Intermountain West: Are We Achieving the Public's Objectives for Forests and Rangelands?

Donna L. Lybecker, Deborah J. Shields, and Michelle Haefele

U.S. Department of Agriculture   Forest Service

Lybecker, Donna L.; Shields, Deborah J.; Haefele, Michelle. 2005. **Survey responses from the Intermountain West: Are we achieving the public's objectives for forests and rangelands?** Gen. Tech. Rep. RMRS-GTR-160. Fort Collins, CO: U.S. Department of Agriculture, Forest Service, Rocky Mountain Research Station. 35 p.

Abstract

The survey on values, objectives, beliefs, and attitudes, implemented as a module of the National Survey on Recreation and the Environment, asked over 7,000 respondents nationwide about their *values* with respect to public lands, *objectives* for the management of these lands, *beliefs* about the role the USDA Forest Service should play in fulfilling those objectives, and *attitudes* about the job the agency has been doing. This report—one of a series of similar regional reports—shows that respondents from the Intermountain West (Arizona, Colorado, Idaho, Montana, Nevada, New Mexico, Utah, Wyoming) are somewhat more strongly in favor of allowing more diverse uses of our forests and grasslands than respondents from the rest of the United States, and slightly less inclined toward protection of ecosystems. Nationwide, as in the Intermountain West, the most important objective was conserving and protecting forests and grassland watersheds.

Other reports in the series *Are We Achieving the Public's Objectives for Forests and Rangelands?*

- *Survey Responses From Region 3* (Arizona and New Mexico) RMRS-GTR-156

- *Survey Responses From Region 5* (California and Hawaii) RMRS-GTR-157

- *Survey Responses From Region 8* (Alabama, Arkansas, Florida, Georgia, Kentucky, Louisiana, Mississippi, North Carolina, Oklahoma, Puerto Rico, South Carolina, Tennessee, Texas, Virginia) RMRS-GTR-158

- *Survey Responses From Region 9* (Connecticut, Delaware, Illinois, Indiana, Iowa, Maine, Maryland, Massachusetts, Michigan, Minnesota, Missouri, New Hampshire, New Jersey, New York, Ohio, Pennsylvania, Rhode Island, Vermont, West Virginia, Wisconsin) RMRS-GTR-159

- Comparison of 2000/2003 Data – Forthcoming

Survey Responses From the Intermountain West: Are We Achieving the Public's Objectives for Forests and Rangelands?

Donna L. Lybecker, Deborah J. Shields, and Michelle Haefele

Contents

Introduction

The mission of the USDA Forest Service is twofold: caring for the land and serving people. Because personal satisfaction is an individual concept having multiple facets, providing high-quality customer service and achieving high levels of customer satisfaction can be as challenging as managing for healthy ecosystems.

A person's attitudes about the Forest Service are often influenced by the nature and outcomes of his or her interactions with Forest Service employees. Were they polite, knowledgeable, helpful, professional? Was the process straightforward, efficient, prompt, and fair? Was the desired outcome achieved, such as acquiring a fuelwood permit or getting information on day hikes? Although traditional customer satisfaction surveys do a good job of collecting this type of information, they tend to focus on delivery of services to specific classes of "users" (for example, permittees or applicants for timber sales or grazing allotments), and are not designed to capture the preferences and attitudes of the broader public.

In addition to personal interactions with the Forest Service, people's perceptions of the agency are also influenced by their attitudes about how and toward what end the Forest Service manages public land. Various segments of the public have both general and in some cases quite detailed objectives related to the health of forests and rangelands, how Forest Service lands should be managed, and the activities that should be allowed to take place on them. If stakeholders observe that an objective they deem important is not being fulfilled, their satisfaction with the Forest Service may be lowered regardless of the quality of their interactions with individual Forest Service employees or their experience with the agency's other protocols. Thus, understanding the public's objectives and comparing them with the agency's objectives can provide useful input to the strategic planning process.

This report describes the public's values, objectives, beliefs, and attitudes for and toward the USDA Forest Service, with particular focus on the Intermountain West region. Information on the public's perceptions has been collected through an ongoing survey entitled "The American Public's Values, Objectives, Beliefs, and Attitudes Regarding Forests and Rangelands" (hereafter VOBA). The VOBA survey asked respondents about their environmental values as they relate to public lands, these objectives for the management of forests and rangelands in general as well as those managed by the Forest Service, their beliefs about whether it is the role of the Forest Service to fulfill these objectives, and their attitudes about the performance of the agency in fulfilling their objectives. This report compares the nation-wide public's response to those from respondents in the Intermountain West. Results show that the public in the Intermountain West region apparently does not view the USDA Forest Service as favorably as does the public in the rest of the United States. This is particularly noteworthy due to the high percentage of public lands in general, and Forest Service lands in particular, within this region.

This report is organized as follows. First there is a brief discussion of the data used in the analysis. The following section outlines the methods used to analyze the American public's values, objectives, beliefs, and attitudes regarding forests and rangelands. Next, results for the Intermountain West region are reported. Finally, the responses from the Intermountain West region are compared with those from the rest of the United States, and with the Southern and Northeastern Regions.

Data and Methodology

Data for this report come from the VOBA survey. The survey was implemented as a module of the National Survey on Recreation and the Environment (NSRE). This random telephone survey was administered for the USDA Forest Service by the University of Tennessee. Although random, it is important to note that a telephone survey such as the NSRE will not adequately represent the views of segments of the population that do not have access to or choose not to have telephones. In addition to the VOBA questions, respondents were asked about their recreational behaviors and basic demographics.

The VOBA part of the survey is comprised of statements to which respondents indicate their level of agreement or approval in four areas—values, objectives, beliefs, and attitudes—regarding forests and rangelands. Respondents indicate their agreement or approval on a five-point scale. The objectives scale items are anchored by 1=not at all important and 5=very important. The Value and Belief scale items are anchored by 1=strongly disagree and 5=strongly agree. The Attitude scale items are anchored by 1=very unfavorable and 5=very favorable.

The VOBA surveys objectives, and related beliefs and attitudes; it does not directly ask respondents about their opinions of the USDA Forest Service goals, as embodied in the Forest Service 2000 Strategic Plan. Likewise, the survey does not ask for an individual's reaction to the Chief's Agenda or Leadership Team priorities. The VOBAs objectives statements were developed during a series of 80 focus group meetings conducted with members of various stakeholder groups as well as individuals throughout the country. As such, they represent the main objectives for land management as they were presented to us by the public.

An objectives hierarchy was constructed for each of the focus groups. These hierarchies indicated the group's goals for the management of forests and rangelands, and how they would like to see each goal or objective achieved. The objectives ranged from the very abstract strategic level to the more focused or applied means level (figure 1).

The strategic-level objectives are abstract, while fundamental level objectives represent a context specific application of strategic objectives. End-state fundamental objectives represent the desired state of the world. Fundamental means objectives capture the methods by which the desired end-state should be achieved.

Objectives elicited from all the focus groups were pooled, duplications eliminated, and overlaps accounted for. Five strategic-level objectives were consistently revealed: Access, Preservation/ Conservation, Economic Development, Education, and Natural Resource Management. The 30 items in the VOBA objectives scale are the fundamental objectives that indicate both end-state

preferences and the means by which they should be achieved. Each correlates to one of the strategic objectives.

Objectives may be applicable only at the regional or national scale, be location specific, or be meaningful at multiple scales. The VOBA survey objectives are applicable to the management of forests and rangelands at a broad geographic scale. Many of the objectives are also meaningful at the regional level. However, the public may have additional objectives specific to home regions that are not captured in the existing national survey instrument. The belief and attitude statements tier down directly from the objectives. For example an objective might be "more hiking trails." The corresponding belief question asks whether the respondent believes that providing more hiking trails is an appropriate role for the USDA Forest Service. The attitude question would then elicit input on the respondent's perception of how well the agency is doing at providing hiking trails.

The value scale in the VOBA survey differs from other value survey instruments in that it focuses on values associated with public lands. It is applicable at multiple spatial scales, and in addition to being used in the national VOBA survey, has been applied at the National Forest scale.

The Public Lands Values scale was developed using approximately 200 items that, through a series of iterations using both student and adult samples around the United States, were reduced to a 25-item scale. This scale was designed to focus on values that people hold for the environment in general and public lands in particular. It has been tested on four National Forests in Colorado (Arapaho, Roosevelt, Pike, and San Isabel) using various traditional and non-traditional stakeholder groups. Research and testing have shown that responses to the Public Lands Values scale can be arranged into two categories: Socially Responsible Individual Values (SRIV) and Socially Responsible Management Values (SRMV).

Finally, it is important to note that the wording of the statements within the VOBA was designed with public lands in mind. Thus some statements may raise questions concerning the appropriateness of the language for private lands. In other words, the language used may not be applicable to some types of private land use concerns, making it less appropriate to draw overarching conclusions about general land management. For example, the objective, "Developing and maintaining continuous trail systems that cross both public and private land for motorized vehicles such as snowmobiles or ATVs," is written with public land managers in mind. A similar objective,

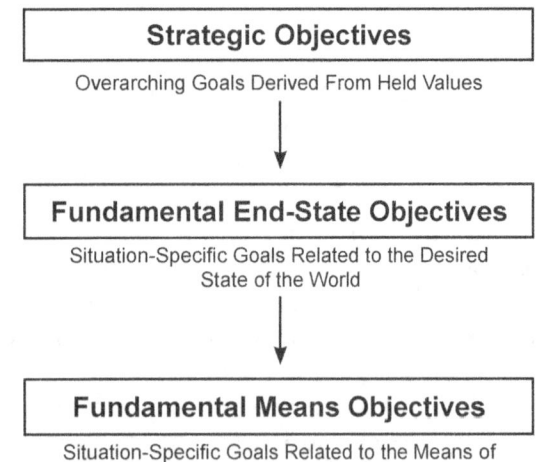

Strategic Objectives

Overarching Goals Derived From Held Values

↓

Fundamental End-State Objectives

Situation-Specific Goals Related to the Desired State of the World

↓

Fundamental Means Objectives

Situation-Specific Goals Related to the Means of Achieving the Desired End-State

Figure 1—Objectives Hierarchy.

written from the perspective of private landowners, might say something like, "Coordinating with public and private actors to support and maintain continuous trail systems that cross both public and private land for motorized vehicles." Although the wording for many of the objectives does not present this concern, it is necessary to remain aware that respondents may be thinking solely of public lands instead of both public and private lands when responding to some of the objectives.[1]

Data Collection

The VOBA survey was implemented as a module of the NSRE, a survey with a nationwide sample. Of the 7,069 nationwide respondents, 638 came from the Intermountain West. The data were collected between late 1999 and early 2000. The number of responses in any region is a function of the overall VOBA sampling design. For each State the size of the sample was proportional to its population. Due to a limited amount of time available for each phone interview, participants were asked to respond to only a portion of the full set of VOBA questions. Each respondent was asked about one fundamental objective from each of the five strategic-level objective categories. Due to this sampling design, each item in the objectives, beliefs, and attitude scales has fewer than the full 638 respondents.

The overall goal of this split sampling design was to control interview time with respondents, yet collect analytically valuable information. This not only lowers costs, but also reduces respondent burden, which should lead to fewer non-responses and therefore to a better sample quality.[2] To ensure high confidence levels, the full national survey was designed so that there was a minimum of 700 responses for each question. This design generates response numbers for each question that are adequate to support multivariate statistical analysis, and provides a high level of confidence in the results. In the Intermountain West the response numbers for each question ranged from 56 to 494. As a result of this smaller sample size, there is a slightly greater chance the results do not fully reflect the precise traits of the region; however, the sample size is still large enough to give a relatively high level of confidence in the results.

Methodology

The objective of this analysis is to determine the important and unimportant objectives, the perceived appropriateness of roles for the USDA Forest Service, the favorable or unfavorable view of the agency's performance, and the uniformly held socially responsible individual and management values. Descriptive statistics, mean, standard deviation, and frequency distribution, were calculated for each of the 115 objective, belief, and attitude statements. Factor scores (group means) were calculated for the values statements and, where appropriate, items were reverse scored (see Appendix).

The Intermountain West

This report focuses on the Intermountain West region of the United States: Montana, Idaho, Wyoming, Nevada, Utah, Colorado, Arizona, and New Mexico. Although not a single USDA Forest Service Region,[3] these eight States share a number of characteristics and are facing similar economic and social transitions. One of the most important similarities within the Intermountain West region is the extent of public lands within these States.[4] Other similarities include wide-open spaces with the majority of the population living in urban centers, a tradition of boom and bust economies, and expansive and rapid growth and development. Additionally, these States are changing from the so –called "Old West" to the "New West," a transition marked by the traditional extractive economy (mining, logging, and ranching) being surpassed by the service sector (everything from tourism services to telecommuting professionals). Despite these changes, in fact possibly due to these changes, there is an enduring regional trait, a "Code of the West"—a way of thinking and living that differs from other regions of the United States.[5] Included within

---

[1] For more detailed information on the survey, see Shields, D., M. Martin, W. Martin, and M. Haefele. 2002. *Survey Results of the American Public's Values, Objectives, Beliefs, and Attitudes Regarding Forests and Grasslands.* Gen. Tech. Rep. RMRS-GTR-95. Fort Collins, CO: U.S. Department of Agriculture, Forest Service, Rocky Mountain Research Station.

[2] For more information on split sampling designs, see for example, Raghunathan, T.E. and Grizzle, J.E. 1995. "A Split Questionnaire Survey Design," *Journal of the American Statistical Association*, 90: 54-63.

[3] These states are parts of USDA Forest Service Regions 1, 2, 3 and 4.

[4] According to the *Atlas of the New West: Portrait of a Changing Region* (W. Riebsame, H. Gosnell and D. Theobald, eds. 1997. New York: W.W. Norton and Company, p. 58), these states consist of between 28.0% and 32.9% public lands.

[5] See for example, Riebsame, W., H. Gosnell and D. Theobald, eds. 1997. *Atlas of the New West: Portrait of a Changing Region* New York: W.W. Norton and Company, and Brick, P., D. Snow, and S. Van de Wetering, eds. 2001. *Across the Great Divide.* Washington D.C.: Island Press. Riebsame, W., H. Gosnell and D. Theobald, eds, 1997.

this region's "code" or identity is a history of self-sufficiency through cooperation, exemplified by actions such as the Sagebrush Rebellion.[6] These traits unite the eight States of the Intermountain West, and distinguish the region from the rest of the United States. Thus, by treating these States as one region, it is possible to shed light on how this distinct segment of the United States public perceives values, objectives, beliefs, and attitudes about forests and rangelands.

Results for the Intermountain West: Objectives, Beliefs, and Attitudes_____

Results from the Intermountain West respondents to the VOBA national survey are reported first for *objectives*, the extent to which the public believes it is the job of the Forest Service to fulfill the objectives (*beliefs*), and the perception of agency performance in fulfilling these objectives (*attitudes*). These results are grouped as to objectives the Intermountain West public feels are the most important, not important, and moderately important. For each of these groups of objectives the level of consensus (or lack thereof) among the public is also highlighted.

Results for the values are then divided into Socially Responsible Individual Public Lands Values with a high level of agreement among Intermountain West respondents, Socially Responsible Individual Public Lands Values with a low level of agreement among respondents, and Socially Responsible Management Values.

Objectives Identified as Important

For this report, a mean response of 4.00 or greater (out of a possible 5) indicates an objective is important

to the respondents in the Intermountain West. Eleven of the original 30 objectives were thus identified as important. Four of these 11 were further specified as "core" objectives because their response rating has a standard deviation (s.d.) of less than 1.00, indicating that the public is generally in agreement about the importance of these objectives.[7]

Core Important Objectives

The four core objectives for the public in the Intermountain West are presented in detail in table 1. For each of the four core objectives, a histogram compares the distribution of responses for the importance of the objective, the agency role, and customer satisfaction. In each case there is agreement that the objective is important, and that it is an appropriate role for the USDA Forest Service. However, this consistency does not hold when looking at agency performance. None of these objectives shows a public with a "very favorable" or "favorable" (mean above 4.00) view of the performance of the USDA Forest Service.

Watershed Protection—The VOBA objective deemed the most important by respondents in the Intermountain West is the conservation and protection of lands that are the source of our water resources. This objective has a mean of 4.69 and a standard deviation of 0.78 (table 1; figure 2, which shows the distribution of responses). The mean of 4.44 for the corresponding belief statement also indicates that the public considers the protection of watersheds to be an appropriate role for the USDA Forest Service. This belief has wide consensus as well, indicated by the standard deviation of 0.92. Agency performance is viewed as somewhat favorable, with a mean of 3.76. This rating, however, does not exhibit as much consensus as the objective and belief (s.d. 1.15).

Volunteer programs—Developing volunteer programs to improve the health of forests and grasslands had the second highest importance ranking, with a mean of 4.60. A standard deviation of 0.76 again indicates wide agreement that these programs are important. The respondents also saw the development of such volunteer programs as an appropriate role for the agency (mean

---

[6] The Sagebrush Rebellion began in the 1970s as an organized resistance in the West to Federal public lands policies—the states wanted more control over the federal lands within their boundaries. Since that time, the Sagebrush Rebellion has become an attitude that exists in the West, reflecting the feeling that Federal policies affecting the West were made in the East and without much attention to the conditions and concerns of the West. For more information see such references as: Policy Analysis Staff Group, US Forest Service. c.a. 1980. "Draft Report Concerning Transfer of Western National Forest System Lands to State Ownership, as Proposed by S. 1680." USDA Forest Service; Cawley, R. McGreggor. 1993. Federal Land, Western Anger: The Sagebrush Rebellion and Environmental Politics. Lawrence, KS: University of Kansas Press.

---

[7] General agreement about the importance of these objectives is revealed with the standard deviation. The standard deviation is defined as the average amount by which scores in a distribution differ from the mean; it offers an indication of the spread of the data. For example, when looking at the importance of a given objective, the standard deviation reveals how tightly all the responses are clustered around the mean score for the stated objective. This helps to reveal if there are extreme responses or if most respondents agreed on their rating.

Table 1--Core important objectives for respondents from the Intermountain West.

OBJECTIVE:	Is this an important objective for you? (1=not at all important, 5=very important)	Do you believe that fulfilling this objective is an appropriate role for the USDA Forest Service? (1=strongly disagree, 5=strongly agree)	How favorably do you view the performance of the USDA Forest Service in fulfilling this objective? (1=very unfavorably, 5=very favorably)
Conserving and protecting forests and grasslands that are the source of our water resources, such as streams, lakes, and watershed areas.	4.69 0.78[a] 110[b]	4.44 0.92 127	3.76 1.15 94
Developing volunteer programs to improve forests and grasslands (for example, planting trees, or improving water quality).	4.60 0.76 107	4.42 0.98 109	3.41 1.13 79
Informing the public about recreation concerns on forests and grasslands such as safety, trail etiquette, and respect for wildlife.	4.57 0.88 100	4.44 0.89 96	3.63 1.21 106
Allowing for diverse uses of forests and grasslands such as grazing, recreation, and wildlife habitat.	4.21 0.97 97	4.10 1.08 78	3.59 1.07 76

[a] Standard deviation
[b] Sample size for each item (n)   The sample sizes for each item are less than the full 638 sample since each respondent was asked only a portion of the 115 VOBA questions due to time limitations

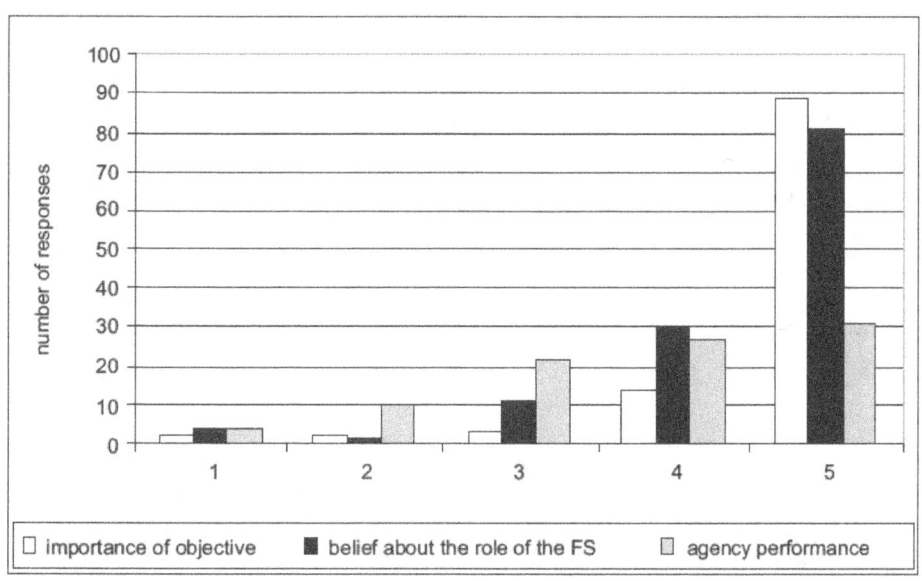

Figure 2—Distribution of Objective, Belief, and Attitude scores for: Conserving and protecting forests and grasslands that are the source of our water resources, such as streams, lakes, and watershed areas.

4.42). Although the standard deviation of 0.98 reveals less agreement than with the objective itself, this belief has wide consensus. Finally, this objective has the lowest performance evaluation of the four core objectives, although the evaluation is still somewhat favorable (mean 3.41). This evaluation also has a high standard deviation (1.13) indicating that the respondents' attitudes vary widely. Figure 3 shows that while the majority of the Intermountain West respondents view agency performance as adequate, fully 80% (the percentage of

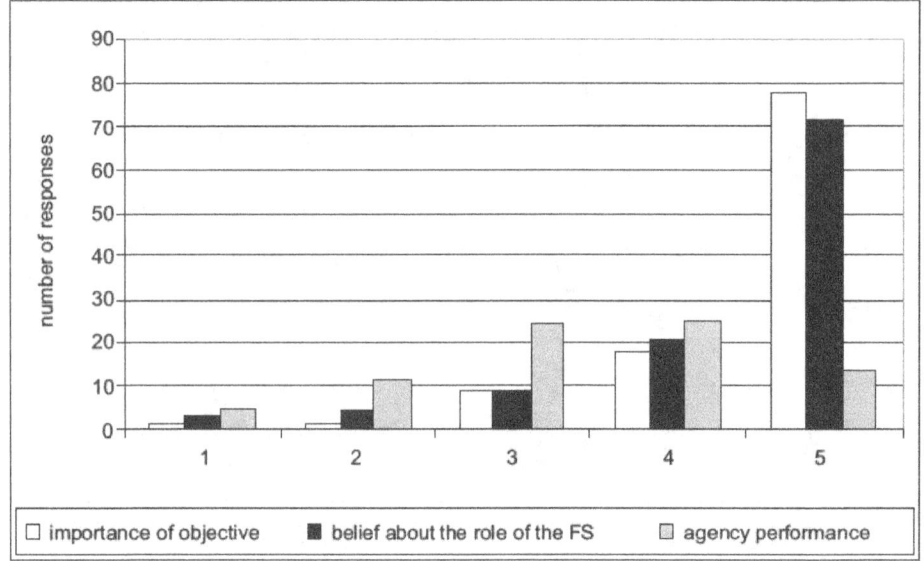

Figure 3—Distribution of Objective, Belief, and Attitude scores for: Developing volunteer programs to improve forests and grasslands (for example, planting trees, or improving water quality).

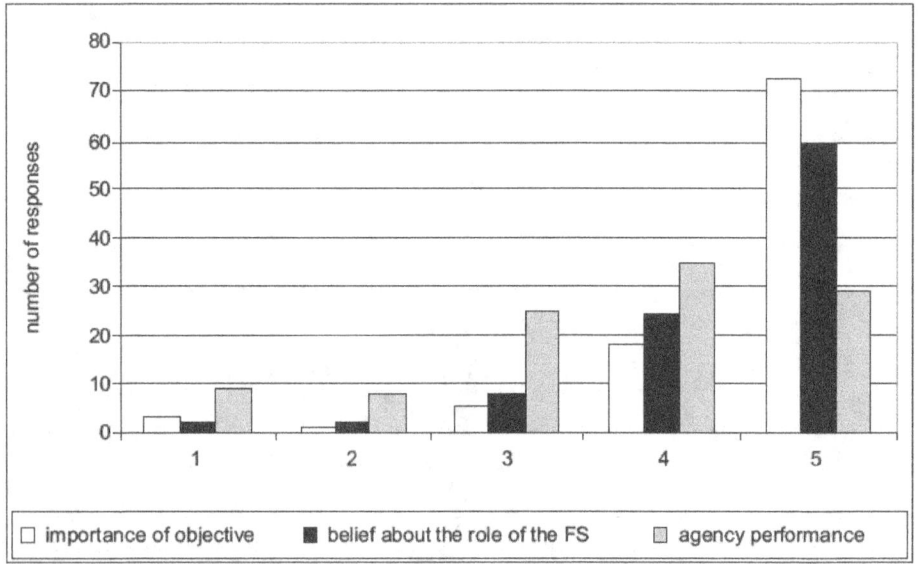

Figure 4—Distribution of Objective, Belief, and Attitude scores for: Informing the public about recreation concerns on forests and grasslands such as safety, trail etiquette, and respect for wildlife.

respondents answering 4 or less) feel that the agency could be doing a better job.

Recreation concerns—The public in the Intermountain West sees distribution of information about recreation concerns as very important (figure 4), with a mean of 4.57. The standard deviation of 0.88 indicates general consensus about the importance of this core objective. The distribution of this type of information is also viewed as an appropriate role for the agency, and this is widely agreed to be the case (mean 4.44, s.d. 0.89). Agency performance is somewhat high (with a mean of 3.63), but there is wide disagreement (s.d. 1.21) about

the appropriateness of the performance. Only a small number of respondents rate the performance of the USDA Forest Service as unfavorable.

Diverse uses—Allowing for diverse uses is seen as an important objective by most respondents (mean 4.21, s.d. 0.97). As with the distribution of recreation information, the Intermountain West respondents see this is an appropriate role for the USDA Forest Service (mean 4.10), but with somewhat less agreement (s.d. 1.08), possibly indicating that some respondents would prefer to see the agency limit uses allowed within forests and grasslands. Agency performance is viewed as somewhat favorable,

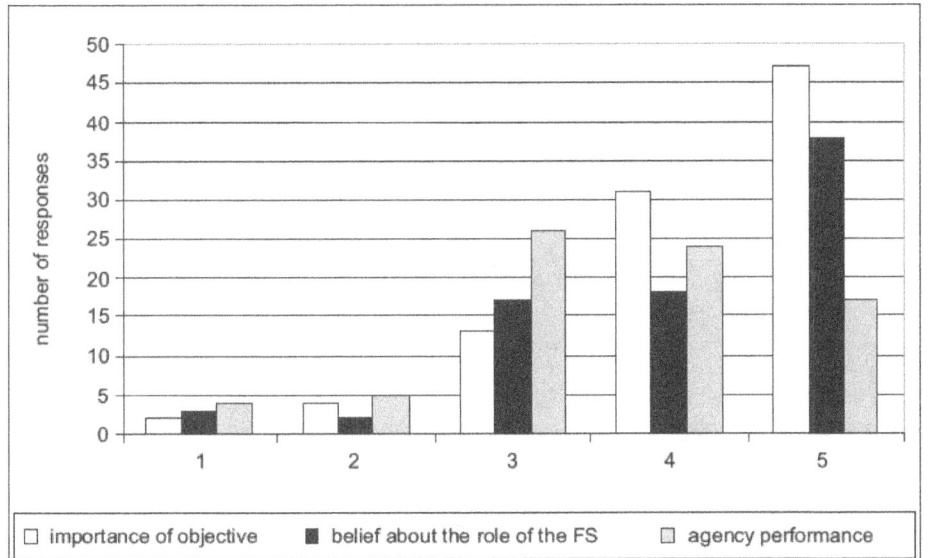

Figure 5—Distribution of Objective, Belief, and Attitude scores for: Allowing for diverse uses of forests and grasslands such as grazing, recreation, and wildlife habitat.

☐ importance of objective   ■ belief about the role of the FS   ☐ agency performance

with a mean of 3.59, but there are some dissenting voices as indicated by the standard deviation (1.07). Figure 5 shows that while the majority of respondents view the objective as important and its fulfillment as an appropriate role for the agency, more than 75% (the percentage of respondents answering 4 or less) felt that the agency could be doing a better job.

Other Important Objectives

Table 2 shows the results for the next seven objectives the respondents in the Intermountain West felt were important. Although these objectives also had means over 4.00, these means have higher standard deviations, indicating that the responses are more diverse. The objectives in table 2 are ordered from those with the lowest standard deviation (higher consensus) to those with higher standard deviations (less consensus). As a result, objectives identified as relatively more important sometimes fall lower in the table than some objectives identified as relatively less important. Each of these objectives will be discussed briefly, but histograms will only be presented for those that exhibit striking disparities in the responses to the importance, beliefs about the role of the USDA Forest Service, and customer satisfaction.

Protection of ecosystems—This objective has a mean of 4.32 and a standard deviation of 1.05, indicating some consensus, although less than for the core objectives. The public in the Intermountain West sees this as an appropriate role for the USDA Forest Service (mean 4.34), but there are some dissenting voices as indicated

by the standard deviation (1.02). Agency performance is seen as somewhat favorable (mean 3.59), but again with some disagreement (s.d. 1.20).

Making decisions locally—The issue of local control is also important to the people of the Intermountain West (mean 4.31), although there is a lower level of agreement (s.d. 1.07). Making it possible for management decisions to be made locally is seen as an appropriate role for the agency (mean 4.22), but with some disagreement (s.d. 1.08). Agency performance is seen as somewhat favorable (mean 3.13), although the high standard deviation (1.50) indicates substantial disagreement. This disagreement suggests that some people in the Intermountain West still support the ideas of the Sagebrush Rebellion—that management decisions should be made locally—and therefore transferring decision making is an appropriate role for the Forest Service, but that the Agency needs to give up more control. Figure 6 shows the familiar correspondence between the importance of the objective and the appropriateness of the agency's role. However, the level of customer satisfaction reveals a third of the public giving an unfavorable rating.

Developing volunteer programs—Development of volunteer programs for trail maintenance and other facility improvements is important to the Intermountain West public (mean 4.16). These respondents are not all in agreement, as indicated by the standard deviation of 1.07. Most respondents feel that the development of these programs is an appropriate role for the USDA Forest Service (mean 4.17, s.d. 1.01). Agency performance

Table 2--Other important objectives for the Intermountain West public.

OBJECTIVE:	Is this an important objective for you? *(1=not at all important, 5=very important)*	Do you believe that fulfilling this objective is an appropriate role for the USDA Forest Service? *(1=strongly disagree, 5=strongly agree)*	How favorably do you view the performance of the USDA Forest Service in fulfilling this objective? *(1=very unfavorably, 5=very favorably)*
Protecting ecosystem and wildlife habitats.	4.32 *1.05*[a] 116[b]	4.34 *1.02* 102	3.59 *1.20* 104
Making management decisions concerning the use of forests and grasslands at the local level rather than at the national level.	4.31 *1.07* 80	4.22 *1.08* 73	3.13 *1.50* 68
Developing volunteer programs to maintain trails and facilities on forests and grasslands (for example, trail maintenance or campground maintenance).	4.16 *1.07* 93	4.17 *1.01* 96	3.61 *1.22* 75
Informing the public on the economic value received by developing our natural resources.	4.01 *1.07* 86	4.06 *1.16* 77	2.73 *1.33* 80
Informing the public on the potential environmental impacts of all uses associated with forests and grasslands.	4.12 *1.08* 82	4.38 *0.95* 92	3.22 *1.39* 90
Developing a national policy that guides natural resource development of all kinds (for example, specifies levels of extraction, and regulates environmental impacts).	4.16 *1.23* 101	3.99 *1.18* 90	3.22 *1.22* 74
Preserving the ability to have a 'wilderness' experience on forests and grasslands.	4.03 *1.25* 98	3.90 *1.32* 114	3.80 *1.05* 126

[a] Standard deviation

[b] Sample size for each item (n) The sample sizes for each item are less than the full 638 sample since each respondent was asked only a portion of the 115 VOBA questions due to time limitations

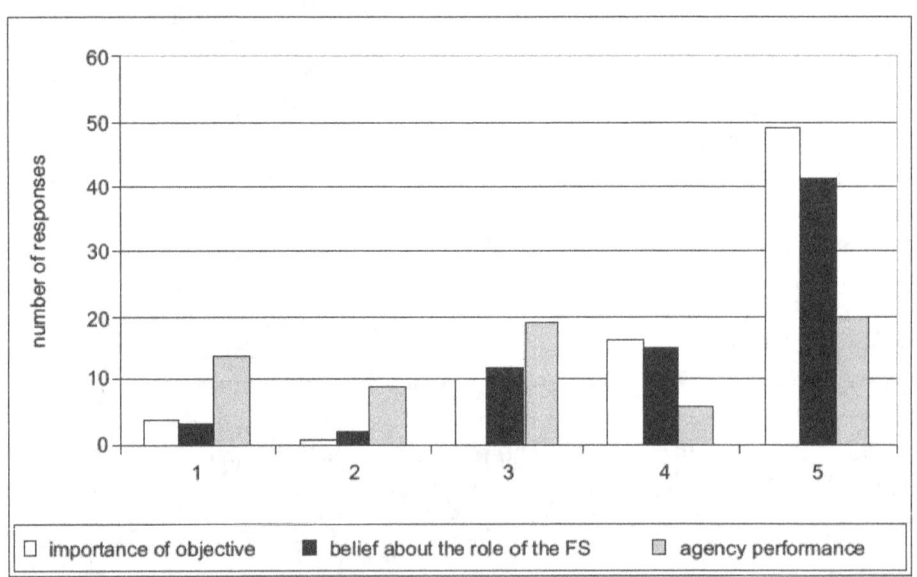

Figure 6—Distribution of Objective, Belief, and Attitude scores for: Making management decisions concerning the use of forests and grasslands at the local level rather than at the national level.

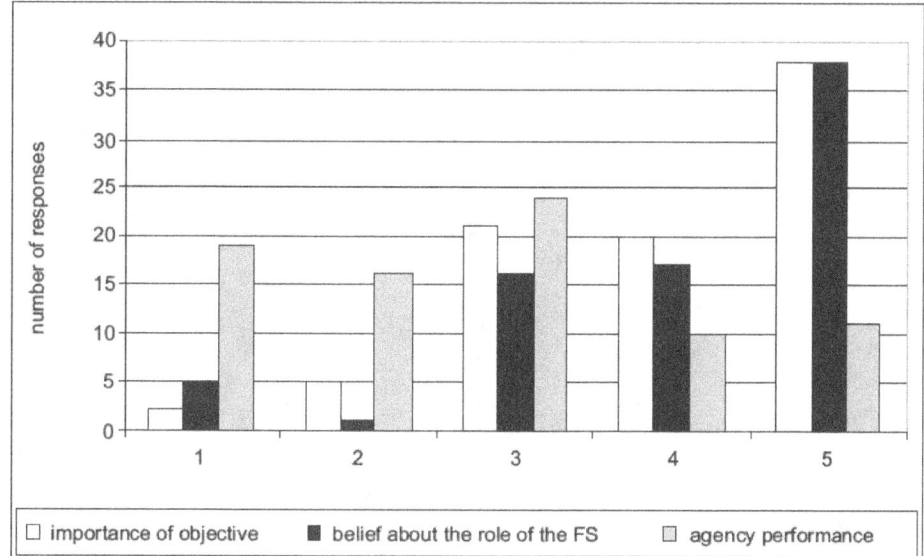

Figure 7—Distribution of Objective, Belief, and Attitude scores for: Informing the public on the economic value received by developing our natural resources.

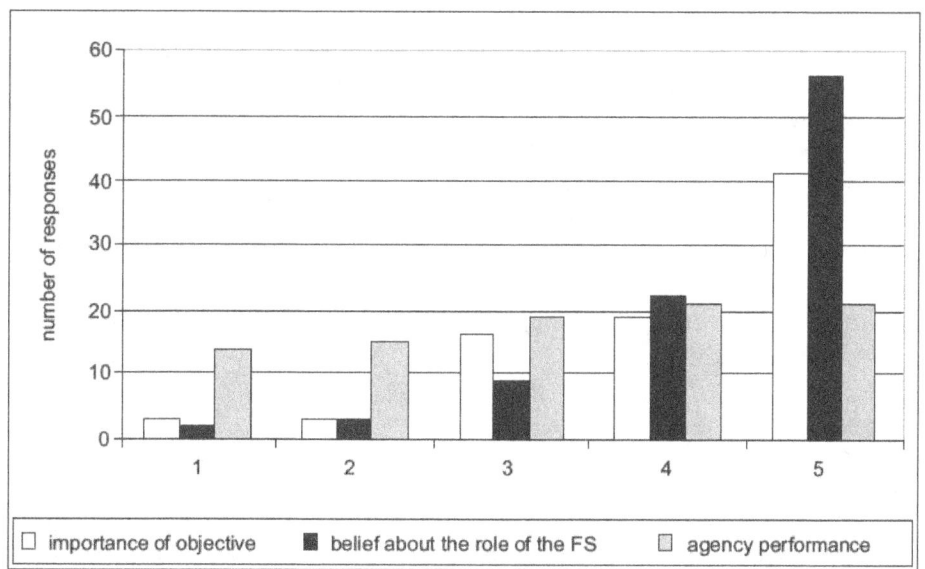

Figure 8—Distribution of Objective, Belief, and Attitude scores for: Informing the public on potential environmental impacts of all uses associated with forest and grasslands.

is seen as somewhat favorable (mean 3.61), although the standard deviation (1.22) again indicates a high level of disagreement.

Informing the public—Two important objectives deal with informing the public. The first of these, informing the public on the economic value received by developing our natural resources, scored a mean of 4.01. This objective has a lower level of agreement, however (s.d. 1.07), indicating there are some members who do not hold this view. Most respondents feel that the development of these programs is an appropriate role for the agency as well (mean 4.06, s.d. 1.16). Agency performance on informing the public about these economic values is seen

as slightly unfavorable (mean 2.73), but again a high standard deviation (1.33) shows that this evaluation is not universal. Figure 7 shows nearly three-fourths of the Intermountain West public views agency performance as neutral or unfavorable.

The second objective dealing with informing the public concerns the potential environmental impacts of all uses associated with forests and grasslands (mean 4.12) (figure 8). As seen with many of these important objectives, the somewhat high standard deviation (1.08) indicates a number of respondents who do not see this as important. Intermountain West respondents are in relative agreement that the provision of such

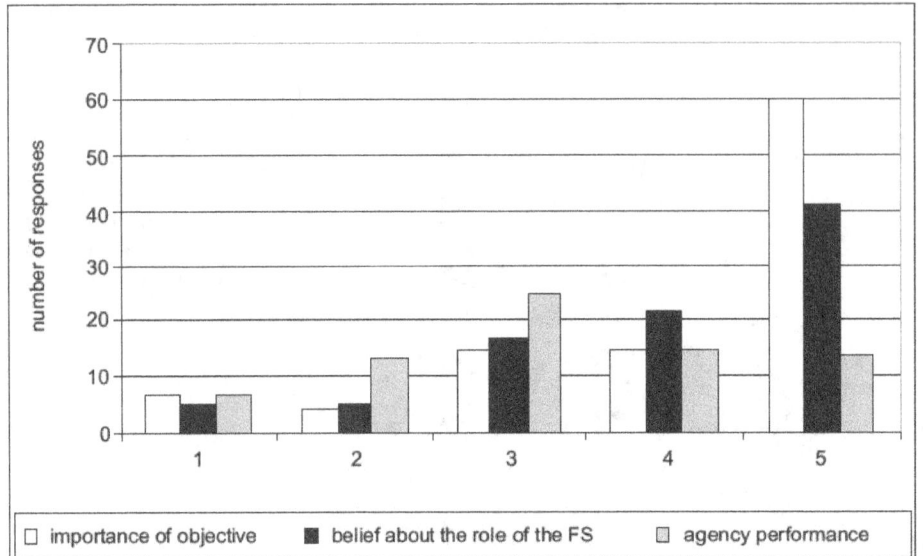

Figure 9—Distribution of Objective, Belief, and Attitude scores for: Developing a national policy that guides natural resources development of all kinds.

opportunities is an appropriate role for the agency (mean 4.38, s.d. 0.95). Finally, the USDA Forest Service is seen as doing a somewhat adequate job providing the public with information on potential environmental impacts (mean 3.22), but again there is less consensus for this evaluation (s.d. 1.39). The histogram (figure 8) reveals that while the majority of the respondents view the objective as important and its fulfillment as an appropriate role for the agency, the distribution of opinions about agency performance is spread more evenly across the range of attitudes.

National policy on resource development—While local decisions are important to the people of the Intermountain West, they also see the need for national level guidance when managing the development of natural resources (mean 4.16) (figure 9). However, the high standard deviation (1.23) may indicate that there are also those who favor a more "hands off" approach from the Washington Office, again representative of the Sagebrush Rebellion sentiment. The development of such national policies is seen as an appropriate role for the agency, although again a high level of disagreement exists (mean 3.99, s.d. 1.18). Agency performance is somewhat favorable, but as has been the case with many other objectives, there is a low level of consensus on the performance of this objective (mean 3.22, s.d. 1.22). Figure 9 illustrates the lack of consensus in the evaluation of agency performance, and shows that while most respondents agree that this objective is important and an appropriate role for the USDA Forest Service, there are also a good many who do not.

Preserving the wilderness experience—Finally, preserving the ability to have a "wilderness" experience on forests and grasslands is another important objective for the people of Intermountain West, although again there is a low level of consensus (mean 4.03, s.d. 1.32). Fulfilling this objective is seen as a somewhat important role for the USDA Forest Service (mean 3.90), although there is less consensus for this evaluation (s.d. 1.25). The agency is evaluated, with a bit more consensus (s.d. 1.05), as doing an adequate job providing the ability to have a wilderness experience (mean 3.80).

Objectives Identified as Not Important

Some objectives in the VOBA were not important to the people of the Intermountain West. These objectives have a mean importance ranking of less than 3.00 (3.00 is the midpoint of the scale, indicating a neutral position). While the means for these means indicate that most respondents did not feel they were important, all of these objectives also exhibit high standard deviations, indicating that there are supporters as well. Divergent evaluations are not surprising since these objectives were included in the VOBA survey based upon the input of the focus groups, some of which were comprised of specific stakeholder groups (and thus may have had strong preferences for these objectives). In other words, while the general public does not feel that these objectives are important, there is a vocal minority that does. These less important objectives are presented in table 3.

Table 3 – Objectives that the Intermountain West respondents do not view as important.

OBJECTIVE:	Is this an important objective for you? *(1=not at all important, 5=very important)*	Do you believe that fulfilling this objective is an appropriate role for the USDA Forest Service? *(1=strongly disagree, 5=strongly agree)*	How favorably do you view the performance of the USDA Forest Service in fulfilling this objective? *(1=very unfavorably, 5=very favorably)*
Developing new paved roads on forests and grasslands for access for cars and recreational vehicles.	2.38 *1.30*[a] 80[b]	2.33 *1.35* 92	3.14 *1.20* 74
Expanding access for motorized off-highway vehicles on forests and grasslands (for example, snowmobiling or 4-wheel driving).	2.60 *1.55* 92	2.52 *1.40* 100	2.88 *1.30* 75
Expanding commercial recreation on forests and grasslands (for example, ski areas, guide services, or outfitters).	2.80 *1.24* 81	2.92 *1.40* 106	3.38 *1.05* 56
Making the permitting process easier for some established uses of forests and grasslands such as grazing, logging, mining, and commercial recreation.	2.93 *1.37* 86	2.86 *1.47* 84	2.87 *1.25* 71
Developing and maintaining continuous trail systems that cross both public and private land for motorized vehicles such as snowmobiles or ATVs.	2.94 *1.46* 90	2.86 *1.50* 93	2.96 *1.17* 78

[a] Standard deviation

[b] Sample size for each item (n) The sample sizes for each item are less than the full 638 sample since each respondent was asked only a portion of the 115 VOBA questions due to time limitations

Access for motorized recreation—Two objectives dealing with access for motorized recreation can be deemed "unimportant" for respondents from the Intermountain West. Developing new paved roads had a low mean of 2.38, but with evidence that there are also some for whom it is important (s.d. 1.30). Likewise, the development of paved roads is not seen by most to be an appropriate role for the USDA Forest Service (mean 2.33), but there is a great deal of disagreement (s.d. 1.35). Finally, the USDA Forest Service is seen as doing a somewhat favorable job in developing new paved roads (mean 3.14), but again there is little consensus (s.d. 1.20). In the histogram for this objective (figure 10) we see that while most people in the Intermountain West do not view the development of new paved roads as important, a good many do feel it is important or at least neutral. Figure 10 also shows that the responses on agency performance are widely distributed.

Expanding off-highway motorized access (figure 11) is also somewhat unimportant to many of the people of the Intermountain West. Again there is very little consensus for this objective (mean 2.60, s.d. 1.55) indicating a constituency for whom such access is more important. Overall, the public does not see the provision of such access as an appropriate role for the Forest Service (mean 2.52), although there are many who do, as indicated by the high standard deviation (1.40). Agency performance on the provision of off-highway motorized access is seen as slightly unfavorable (mean 2.88), but again this evaluation is not universal (s.d. 1.30). Figure 11 summarizes that while a majority of respondents in the Intermountain West feel that expanding off-highway motorized access is not important and, further, that such expansion is not an appropriate activity for the agency, a large number feel it is important and many are neutral. The histogram also shows that, as with the development of new paved roads, customer satisfaction varies considerably among respondents.

Expanding commercial recreation—Expanding commercial recreation on forests and grasslands is not viewed by most of the Intermountain West public as an important objective (mean 2.80), although the high standard deviation (1.24) indicates some exceptions. Nor is it seen as an appropriate role for the agency (mean

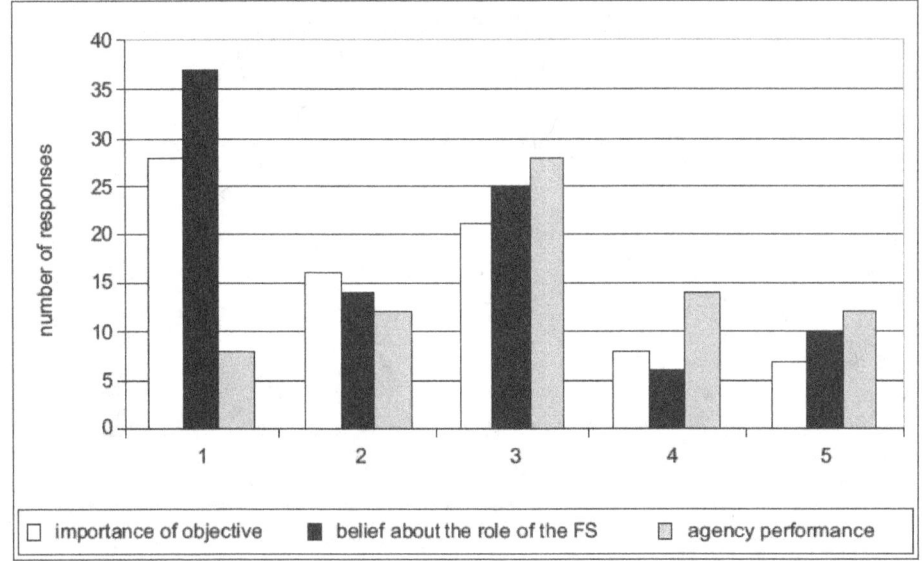

Figure 10—Distribution of Objective, Belief, and Attitude scores for: Developing new paved roads on forests and grasslands for access for cars and recreational vehicles.

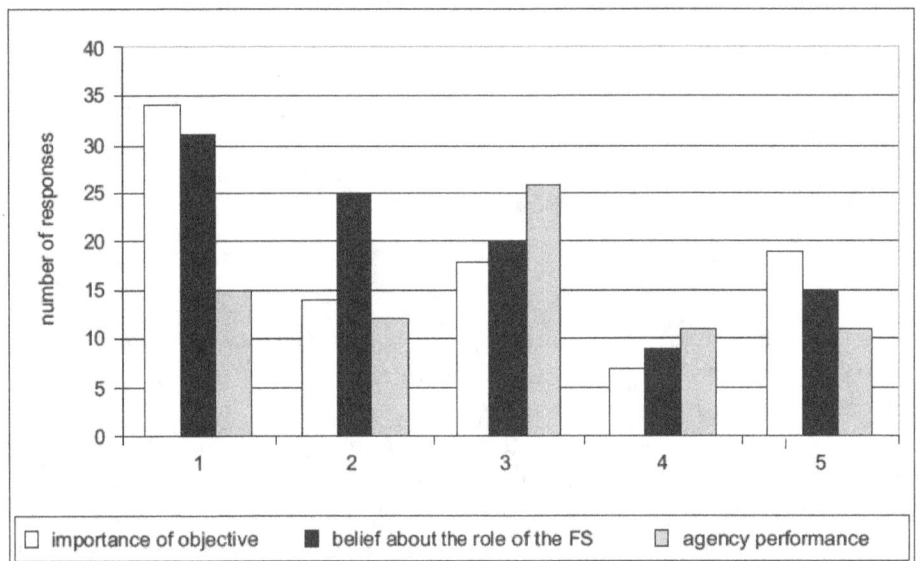

Figure 11—Distribution of Objective, Belief, and Attitude scores for: Expanding access for motorized off-highway vehicles on forests and grasslands (for example, snowmobiling or 4-wheel driving)

2.92), although this opinion is not universally agreed upon, as indicated by a standard deviation of 1.40. The performance of the Forest Service in expanding commercial recreation is seen as somewhat favorable (mean 3.38), although there is some disagreement (s.d. 1.05). Figure 12 shows that the majority of respondents are neutral about the importance of this objective and agency performance. The evaluation of expanding commercial recreation as an appropriate activity for the agency is fairly evenly spread among the responses. These responses may indicate that while there are a minority for whom this objective strikes a chord (either as important or unimportant), the general public is not as interested in (or is perhaps unaware of) the issue.

Easing the permitting process—Making the permitting process easier for some established uses of forest and grassland (grazing, logging, mining, and commercial recreation) is not viewed by most respondents from the Intermountain West as an important issue (mean 2.93). Again, however, the high standard deviation for this objective (1.37) indicates there may be some groups who do view this as an important objective. Likewise, making the permitting process easier for established uses is not seen by most in the Intermountain West as

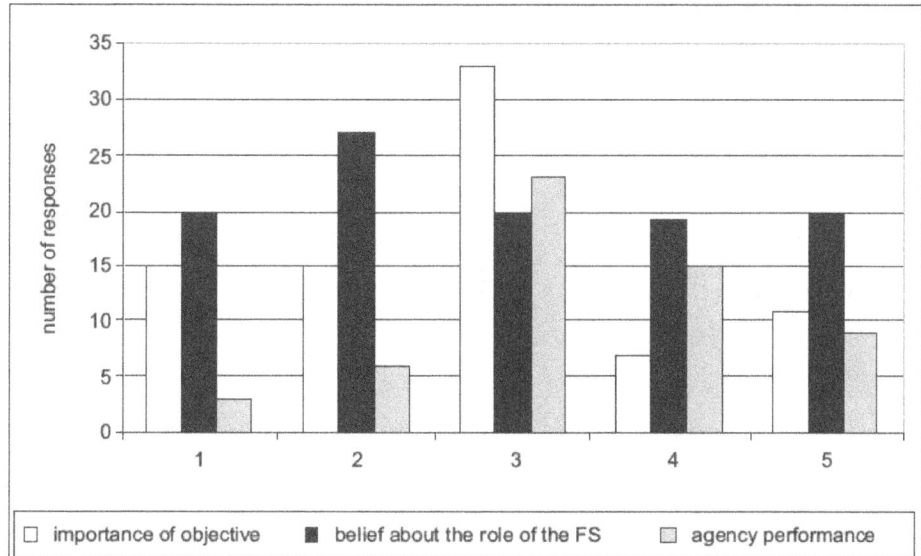

Figure 12—Distribution of Objective, Belief, and Attitude scores for: Expanding commercial recreation on forests and grasslands (for example, ski areas, guide services, or outfitters).

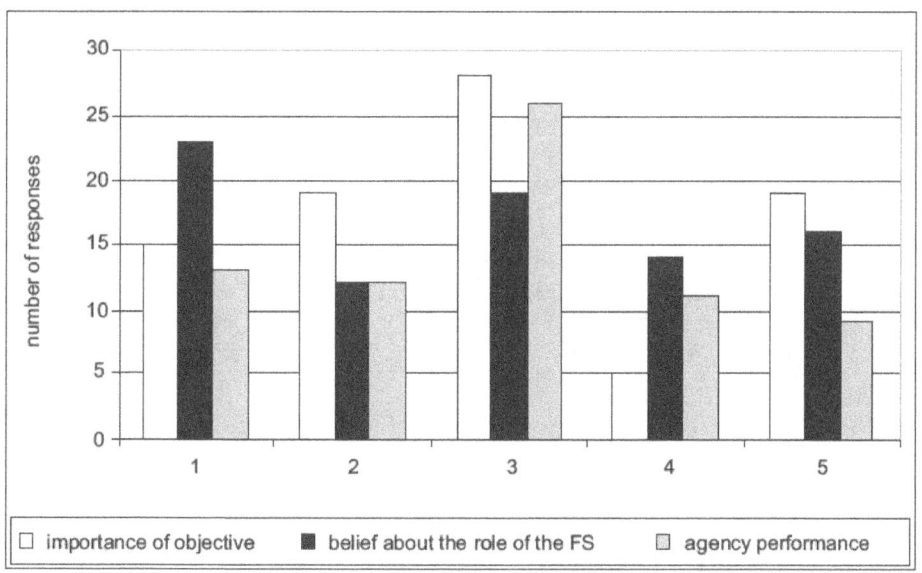

Figure 13—Distribution of Objective, Belief, and Attitude scores for: Making the permitting process easier for some established uses of forests and grasslands such as grazing, logging, mining, and commercial recreation.

an appropriate role for the USDA Forest Service (mean 2.86), but there is little consensus (s.d. 1.47) for this evaluation. Agency performance on the easing of the permitting process for established uses is see as slightly unfavorable (mean 2.87), but, as with the other responses for this objective, this evaluation is not universal (s.d. 1.25). The histogram for this objective (figure 13) resembles the one for expansion of commercial recreation: the majority of respondents were neutral for both the importance of the objective and agency performance, while evaluation of appropriateness of the role for the Forest Service is more wide spread.

Developing trail systems—The issue of developing and maintaining continuous trail systems that cross both public and private land for motorized vehicles such as snowmobiles or ATVs is unimportant to most of the public of the Intermountain West (mean 2.94), but with evidence there are also some for whom it is important (s.d. 1.46). Developing and maintaining such a trail system is not seen by most as an appropriate role for the USDA Forest Service (mean 2.86), although again, there is a lack of agreement as to this role (s.d. 1.50). Agency performance is not seen as favorable, but the standard deviation of 1.17 indicates not all respondents agree (figure 14).

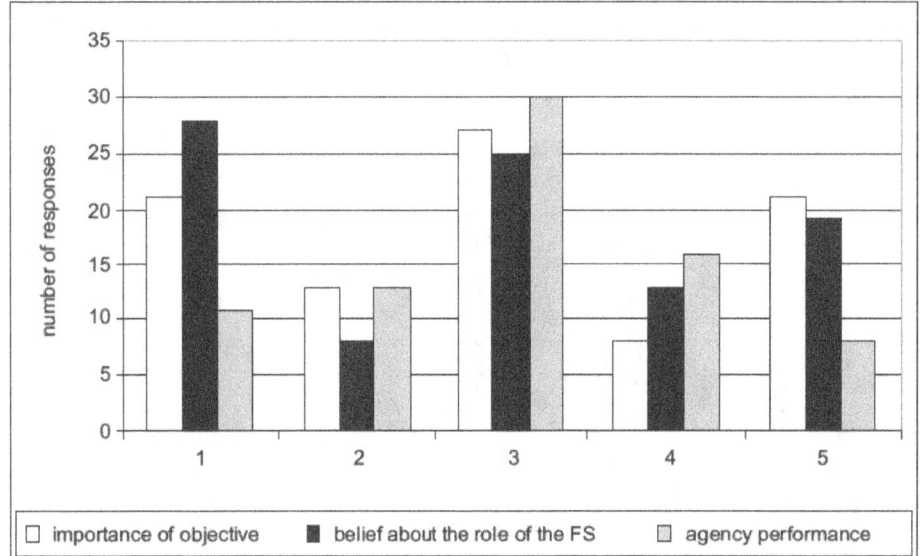

Figure 14—Distribution of Objective, Belief, and Attitude scores for: Developing and maintaining continuous trail systems that cross both public and private land for motorized vehicles such as snowmobiles or ATVs.

Legend: □ importance of objective ■ belief about the role of the FS □ agency performance

Objectives Identified as Moderately Important

Table 4 presents ratings for those objectives the people of the Intermountain West feel are somewhat important, or those for which they are more neutral. Each objective within this set has a mean between 3.00 and 4.00. As with the less important objectives, all of these objectives also have relatively high standard deviations, indicating that while most people do not feel strongly about them, a few do. Results for this group of objectives have been organized to facilitate a discussion of related issues. For example, objectives that deal either directly or indirectly with resource extraction are grouped together. Within these groupings, the objectives are organized in order of decreasing importance.

Resource extraction and use—The preservation of natural preservation of natural resources of forests and grasslands through policies that end timber harvesting and mining is of moderate importance to the Intermountain West (mean 3.86). This objective has a low level of agreement, however, as indicated by the high standard deviation (1.34). The implementation of such restrictions is seen as a somewhat appropriate role for the USDA forest Service (mean 3.65), although the high standard deviation (1.52) indicates there are many who disagree. The USDA Forest Service is doing a somewhat adequate job restricting timber harvesting and grazing, but again there is little consensus with this evaluation (mean 3.32, s.d. 1.28).

Forests and grasslands have many cultural uses by Native Americans and Hispanics, and the preservation of these uses is seen as somewhat important by the Intermountain West respondents (mean 3.82). This opinion is not shared by all within the region, as can be seen in the high standard deviation (1.31). Preserving such cultural uses is seen as a somewhat important role for the USDA Forest Service (mean 3.43), but here again we see a lack of consensus similar to that for the importance of the objective (s.d. 1.31). Agency performance is only somewhat favorable (mean 3.38), although there is more consensus with agency performance than with importance of the objective or appropriateness of the task for the Forest Service (s.d. 1.07).

Wilderness designation can usually be expected to meet with some controversy, and the Intermountain West responses indicate this potential. While the mean for this objective indicates that most people feel it is somewhat important (3.82), the high standard deviation (1.39) also shows a high level of disagreement. The designation of wilderness is seen as an appropriate role for the agency (mean 3.42) although again we see that this is not a universal opinion (s.d. 1.60). In this case the high standard deviation may actually reflect the knowledge that Congress, not the USDA Forest Service, is the body responsible for officially designating wilderness. The USDA Forest Service is seen as performing at a somewhat favorable level, but this evaluation is not consistent (mean 3.01, s.d. 1.37).

Table 4--Objectives of moderate importance for the Intermountain West respondents.

OBJECTIVE:		Is this an important objective for you? *(1=not at all important, 5=very important)*	Do you believe that fulfilling this objective is an appropriate role for the USDA Forest Service? *(1=strongly disagree, 5=strongly agree)*	How favorably do you view the performance of the USDA Forest Service in fulfilling this objective? *(1=very unfavorably, 5=very favorably)*
Resource Extraction and Use	Preserving the natural resources of forests and grasslands through such policies as no timber harvesting or no mining.	3.86 *1.34[a]* 111[b]	3.65 *1.52* 110	3.32 *1.28* 97
	Preserving the cultural uses of forests and grasslands by Native Americans and Native Hispanics[#] such as firewood gathering, herb/berry/plant gathering, and ceremonial uses.	3.82 *1.31* 113	3.43 *1.31* 101	3.38 *1.07* 78
	Designating more wilderness areas on public land that stops access for development and motorized uses.	3.82 *1.39* 109	3.42 *1.60* 91	3.01 *1.37* 80
	Providing natural resources from forests and grasslands to support communities dependent on grazing, mining, or timber harvesting.	3.69 *1.27* 90	3.37 *1.19* 83	3.29 *1.15* 94
	Restricting mineral development on forests and grasslands.	3.55 *1.45* 88	3.78 *1.46* 86	3.04 *1.30* 110
	Restricting timber harvesting and grazing on forests and grasslands.	3.54 *1.56* 90	3.36 *1.49* 97	3.09 *1.30* 69
Public Input & Information	Encouraging collaboration between groups in order to share information concerning uses of forests and grasslands.	3.98 *1.17* 82	4.21 *1.07* 84	3.70 *1.14* 79
	Using public advisory committees to advise on public land management issues.	3.77 *1.17* 70	4.00 *1.15* 74	3.14 *1.09* 59
Recreation	Developing and maintaining continuous trail systems that cross both public and private land for non-motorized recreation such as hiking or cross-country skiing.	3.91 *1.14* 85	3.81 *1.26* 81	3.51 *1.23* 86
	Increasing law enforcement efforts by public land agencies on public lands.	3.76 *1.23* 66	3.62 *1.24* 82	3.41 *1.29* 66
	Designating some existing trails for specific use (for example, creating separate trails for snowmobiling and cross-country skiing or for mountain biking and horseback riding.)	3.76 *1.29* 85	3.87 *1.20* 93	3.23 *1.21* 83
	Paying an entry fee that goes to support public land	3.47 *1.34* 77	3.61 *1.35* 80	3.11 *1.36* 64
Land Acquisition	Increasing the total number of acres in the public land system.	3 39 *1.43* 77	3 70 *1.35* 83	3 25 *1.27* 73
	Allowing public land mangers to trade public lands for private lands (for example, to eliminate private property within public land boundaries, or to acquire unique areas of land).	3.14 *1.54* 71	3.23 *1.26* 78	3.09 *1.24* 66

[a] Standard deviation

[b] Sample size for each item (n) The sample sizes for each item are less than the full 638 sample since each respondent was asked only a portion of the 115 VOBA questions due to time limitations

[#] The term "Native Hispanic" was used in the survey to differentiate Hispanics born in the US from those who moved to the US This term was changed to "traditional groups" in the 2003 survey

Many communities are dependent upon public forests and grasslands for their economic bases. Providing natural resources to these communities is a somewhat important objective for the people of the Intermountain West (mean 3.69), although the importance of this objective is not universally agreed upon as seen by the high standard deviation (1.27). The people of the Intermountain West see the agency role of providing natural resources to dependent communities as somewhat important (mean 3.37), but again there is little consensus (s.d. 1.19). Finally, agency performance in providing these natural resources is rated as somewhat favorable (mean 3.29) and the level of agreement is similar to that seen for the agency role (s.d. 1.15).

Restriction of mineral development on forests and grasslands is similarly considered to be of moderate importance in the Intermountain West (mean 3.55). As with many of the moderately important objectives, there is wide disagreement about the evaluation of this objective (s.d. 1.45). Implementation of such restrictions is seen as a somewhat appropriate role for the USDA Forest Service (mean 3.78), but disagreement is evident (s.d. 1.46). Similarly, agency performance is somewhat favorable (3.04), but with a large disparity of responses (s.d. 1.30).

The last moderately important objective dealing with resources extraction and use is the restriction of timber harvesting and grazing on forests and grasslands (mean 3.54). Again, a high standard deviation (1.56) indicates little consensus in this evaluation of importance. Likewise, the public of the Intermountain West feels that this type of restriction is a somewhat appropriate role for the USDA Forest Service (mean 3.36, s.d. 1.49). Finally, agency performance is somewhat favorable (mean 3.09), but again with a large disparity of responses (s.d. 1.30).

Public input and information—Collaborative management is being applied more and more frequently in Federal land management. The Intermountain West respondents feel that encouraging such collaboration is a moderately important objective (mean 3.98), with some disagreement (s.d. 1.17). These respondents do strongly feel that the Forest Service should be encouraging collaboration (mean 4.21), and there is more agreement about this role for the agency (s.d. 1.07). Agency performance is somewhat favorable (mean 3.70), but again we see a lack of consensus (s.d. 1.14).

Public input into land management decisions is always important to at least some Forest stakeholders. The form for this input can influence how participation takes place and how people feel about the process. In the same spirit as collaboration, many people have advocated using public advisory committees to inform land management decision makers and to provide input into management decisions. The people of the Intermountain West find the use of such committees to be somewhat important, but there is a low level of agreement (mean 3.77, s.d. 1.17). Using such committees is believed to be an appropriate role for the agency, with a degree of agreement similar to that for the importance of the objective (mean 4.00, s.d. 1.15). The performance of the USDA Forest Service is viewed somewhat favorably (mean 3.14, s.d. 1.09).

Recreation—The development of continuous trail systems, crossing both public and private land, for non-motorized access is seen as somewhat important (mean 3.91), but with some disagreement (s.d. 1.14). This may indicate that while many people would like to use such a system, there are also many respondents (perhaps potentially affected landowners) who would see such a system of access as an infringement of property rights. It is also interesting to note that the residents of the Intermountain West find the development of a similar trail system for motorized recreation to be considerably less important (see "Objectives Identified as Not Important by Respondents in the Intermountain West"). The development of a system of private/public non-motorized access is seen as a somewhat appropriate role for the agency (mean 3.81), however again with a level of disagreement (s.d. 1.26). Agency performance is evaluated as somewhat favorable, but as with the other aspects of this objective, this evaluation is not universally held (mean 3.51, s.d. 1.23).

Law enforcement on public lands is moderately important to Intermountain West residents, although some lack of agreement exists (mean 3.76, s.d. 1.23). Respondents believe that increasing law enforcement is a somewhat appropriate role for the USDA Forest Service, but here again there is considerable disagreement (mean 3.62, s.d. 1.24). Agency performance is rated somewhat favorable, but the level of agreement is lower still for this evaluation (mean 3.41, s.d. 1.29).

Conflicts between incompatible recreation uses are often an issue on public lands, including those in the National Forest System. One solution to this type of conflict would be to designate some trails for specific uses (for example separate trails for cross-country skiing and snowmobiling). When asked about the objective of designating specific-use trails, the respondents from the Intermountain West evaluated the objective to be somewhat important, although some disagreement was revealed (mean 3.76, s.d. 1.29). Creating such designations for trails is generally believed to be an appropriate role for the Forest Service (mean 3.87), although this belief is not shared by all respondents (s.d. 1.20). When assessing the performance of the agency, the respondents show a similar level of agreement (s.d. 1.21), and give the agency a somewhat favorable evaluation (mean 3.23).

Most respondents in the Intermountain West region feel that it is somewhat important to pay an entry fee to support public lands (mean 3.47), but as can be expected, there is a lack of consensus on this objective (s.d. 1.34). The people of the Intermountain West do feel that this would be an appropriate role for the agency, but again, there is disagreement (mean 3.61, 1.35). Finally, agency performance is seen as adequate, although there is a lack of consensus (mean 3.11, s.d. 1.36).

Land acquisition—Increasing the total number of acres in the public land system is seen by the Intermountain West population as a somewhat important objective (mean 3.39), but this is a potentially contentious issue due to the evident lack of consensus (s.d. 1.43). Adding to the public domain is seen as an appropriate role for the agency (mean 3.70), but there is also a lack of agreement as to this role (s.d. 1.35) again possibly indicating differences in knowledge about who would actually have the authority to acquire additional public lands. There is also some lack of agreement as to the performance of the agency in increasing public land acreage (s.d. 1.27), but the people of the Intermountain West give the Forest Service a somewhat adequate rating (mean 3.25).

Finally, allowing public land managers to trade public lands for private lands is a somewhat important objective for Intermountain West residents, but this objective is far from universally supported (mean 3.14, s.d. 1.54). The USDA Forest Service is viewed as an appropriate agency to fulfill this objective, although not all groups view it as such (mean 3.23, s.d. 1.26). Agency performance is viewed as somewhat favorable, with a mean of 3.09 and standard deviation of 1.24

Results for the Intermountain West: Public Lands Values_____

Previous research using the Public Lands Values Scale has shown that items consistently fall into two categories. The first category, which deals with individual actions or values, has been labeled Socially Responsible Individual Values (tables 5 and 6). For these values, a higher mean indicates a higher level of environmental orientation. The second category, which deals with how public lands should be managed, has been labeled Socially Responsible Management Values (table 7). These values statements are worded so that a

Table 5--Socially responsible individual public lands values for the Intermountain West with a high level of agreement among respondents.

Values *(1=strongly disagree. 5=strongly agree)*	Mean
I am glad there are National Forests even if I never get to see them.	4.74 *0.74*[a] 189[b]
Manufacturers should be encouraged to use recycled materials in their manufacturing and processing operations.	4.63 *0.80* 156
People should be more concerned about how our public lands are used.	4.46 *0.97* 164
Future generations should be as important as the current one in the decisions about public lands.	4.45 *0.97* 185
Consumers should be interested in the environmental consequences of the products they purchase.	4.38 *0.97* 158
Donating time or money to worthy causes is important to me.	4.20 *0.97* 172

[a] Standard deviation

[b] Sample size for each item (n) The sample sizes for each item are less than the full 638 sample since each respondent was asked only a portion of the 115 VOBA questions due to time limitations

Table 6--Socially responsible individual public lands values for the Intermountain West with a low level of agreement among respondents.

Values *(1=strongly disagree, 5=strongly agree)*	Mean
People can think public lands are valuable even if they never go there themselves.	4.48 *1.00*[a] 180[b]
I am willing to make personal sacrifices for the sake of slowing down pollution.	4.27 *1.01* 155
People should urge their friends to limit their use of products made from scarce resources.	4.04 *1.21* 181
I have often thought that if we could just get by with a little less there would be more left for future generations.	3.94 *1.23* 157
I am willing to stop buying products from companies that pollute the environment even though it might be inconvenient.	3.86 *1.25* 169
Forests have a right to exist for their own sake, regardless of human concerns and uses.	3.96 *1.29* 166
Natural resources should be preserved even if people must do without some products.	3.83 *1.34* 191
The whole pollution issue has never upset me too much since I feel it's somewhat overrated. [c]	2.27 *1.36* 166
Wildlife, plants, and humans have equal rights to live and grow.	4.05 *1.38* 158
I would be willing to sign a petition for an environmental cause.	3.61 *1.50* 163
I would be willing to pay five dollars more each time I use public lands for recreational purposes (for example, hiking, camping, hunting).	3.02 *1.54* 211

[a] Standard deviation

[b] Sample size for each item (n) The sample sizes for each item are less than the full 638 sample since each respondent was asked only a portion of the 115 VOBA questions due to time limitations

[c] This value statement has been reverse scored to make the responses consistent with the other statements For a more complete discussion of reverse scoring, please refer to the appendix

higher value indicates that relatively more importance is placed upon human uses of, or commodity production from, forests and grasslands.

Socially Responsible Individual Values

Most of the means for these values indicate an environmental orientation in the people of the Intermountain West. For many of the values statements, however, the standard deviation indicates that the level of agreement is low. Responses to the Socially Responsible Individual Values are therefore broken into two groups, those for which there is a high degree of consensus and those for which the level of agreement is lower (based upon the standard deviation).

Socially Responsible Individual Values With a High Degree of Consensus

It is interesting to note (table 5) that when Socially Responsible Individual Values with a higher degree of agreement (standard deviation of 1.00 or less) are placed in order of increasing standard deviation, the order of agreement is almost analogously decreasing. In other words, the values statements with higher means (indicating more environmentally oriented values) are also those with higher levels of consensus.

Socially Responsible Individual Values With a Low Degree of Consensus

Table 6 shows the values statements with lower consensus among the respondents. These again nearly

Table 7--Socially responsible management public lands values for the Intermountain West.

Values (1=strongly disagree. 5=strongly agree)	Mean
The Federal government should subsidize the development and leasing of public lands to companies.	1.93 *1.20*[a] 207[b]
I think that the public land managers are doing an adequate job of protecting natural resources from being overused.	3.03 *1.21* 190
The decision to develop resources should be based mostly on economic grounds.	2.70 *1.29* 192
The primary use of forests should be for products that are useful to humans.	2.47 *1.30* 238
The government has better places to spend money than devoting resources to a strong conservation program.	2.38 *1.39* 194
The most important role for the public lands is providing jobs and income for local people.	2.76 *1.40* 232
The main reason for maintaining resources today is so we can use them in the future if we need to.	2.48 *1.41* 211
We should actively harvest more trees to meet the needs of a much larger human population.	2.70 *1.51* 205

[a] Standard deviation

[b] Sample size for each item (n) The sample sizes for each item are less than the full 638 sample since each respondent was asked only a portion of the 115 VOBA questions due to time limitations

always exhibit the characteristic that higher levels of environmental orientation also correspond to higher consensus (even among these values with low consensus).

Figure 15 shows the responses to the statement "I would be willing to pay $5 more each time I use public lands for recreational purposes." While many respondents agree with this statement (the mean is 3.02), there is a noticeable amount of disagreement (indicated by the high standard deviation of 1.54). The figure shows that there is an identifiable minority who clearly disagree. Since fees are often a reality in order to provide such recreation opportunities, it is important to be aware that while most support them, such policies will also most likely meet with considerable resistance.

Socially Responsible Management Values

The results for the Socially Responsible Management Values (table 7) are presented in order from higher agreement to lower agreement. As the previous section demonstrates, although most people believe in protecting the environment, disagreement arises about the appropriate methods to achieve such protection. The differences in responses to this set of values are likely the basis for disagreement noted in some of the aforementioned objectives. Histograms are presented for each of the Socially Responsible Management Values, but only the first value is discussed because of its direct relevance to customer satisfaction.

It is interesting to note the low level of agreement with the statement "The Federal government should subsidize the development and leasing of public lands to companies." Furthermore, although there is a relatively high level of disagreement among the respondents in the Intermountain West regarding this statement, there is more agreement for this statement than any of the other Socially Responsible Management Public Lands Values. Figure 16 shows the responses to this statement. Figures 17 through 23 show responses to the other seven "Management Values" statements.

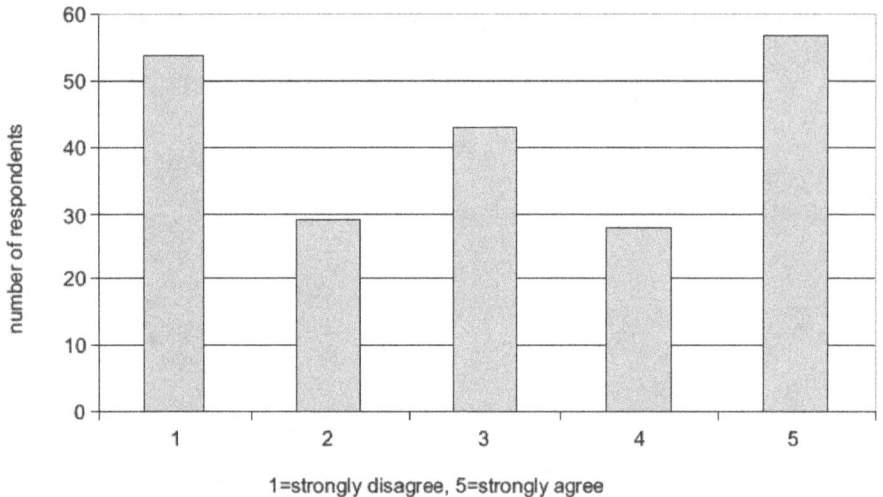

Figure 15—Distribution of responses to: "I would be willing to pay five dollars more each time I use public lands for recreational purposes (for example, hiking, camping, hunting)."

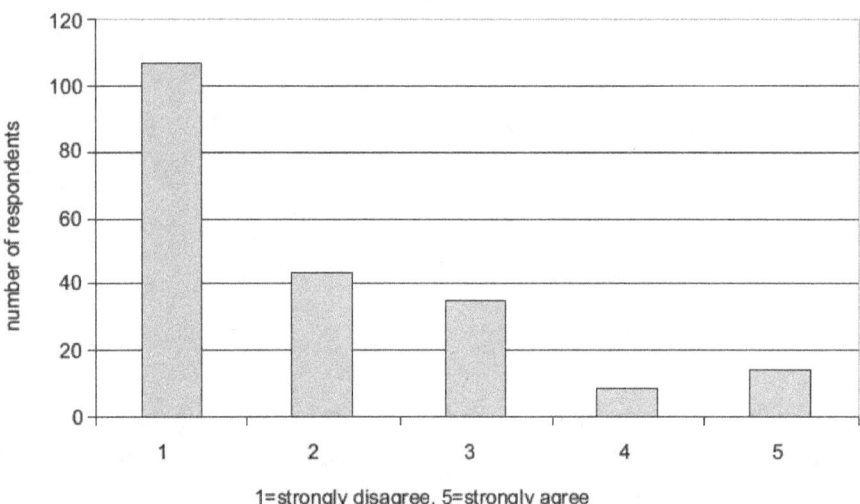

Figure 16—Distribution of responses to: "The Federal government should subsidize the development and leasing of public lands to companies."

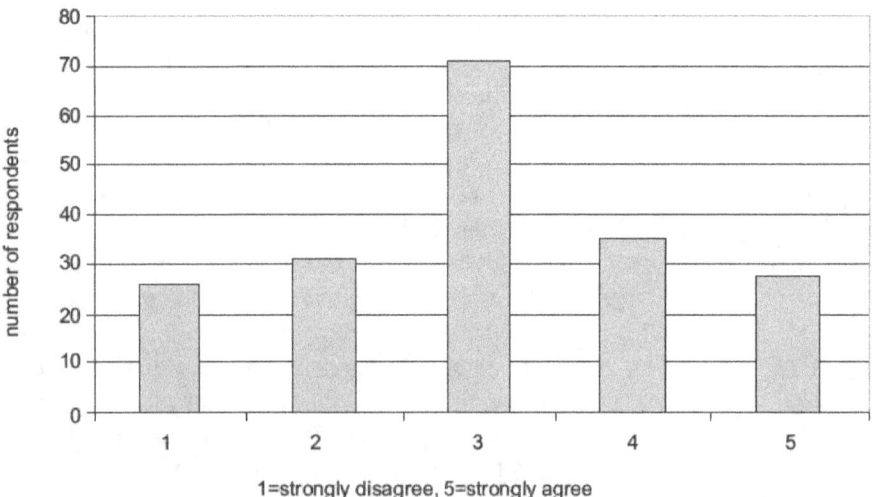

Figure 17—Distribution of responses to: "I think that the public land managers are doing an adequate job of protecting natural resources from being overused."

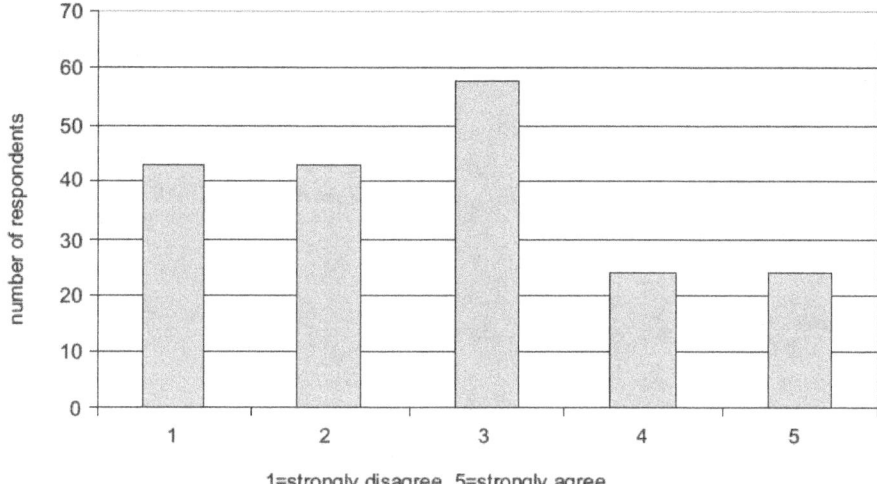

Figure 18—Distribution of responses to: "The decision to develop resources should be based mostly on economic grounds."

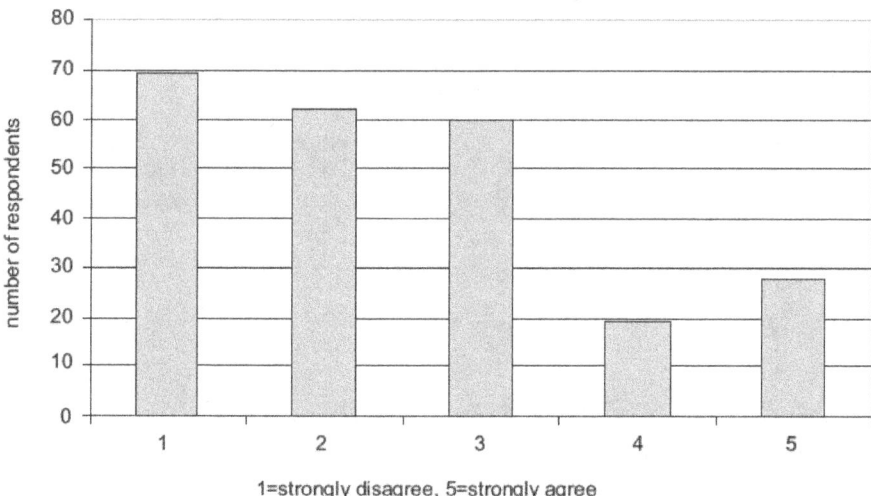

Figure 19—Distribution of responses to: "The primary use of forests should be for products that are useful to humans."

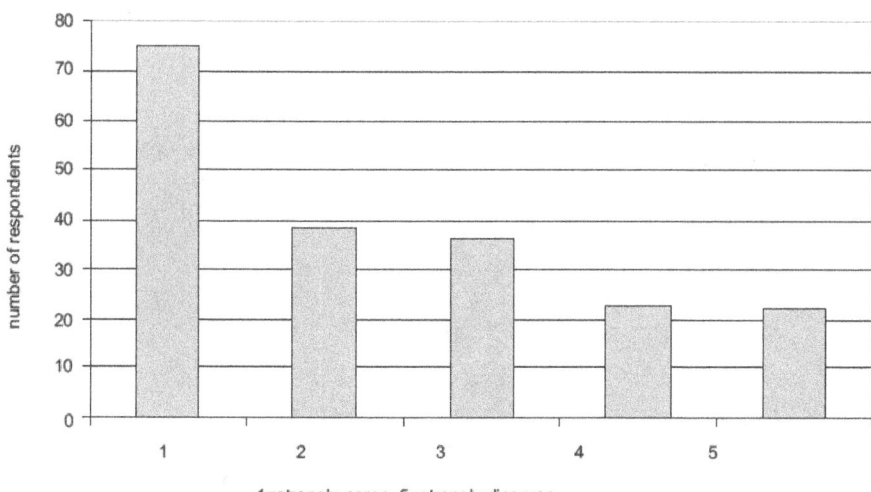

Figure 20—Distribution of responses to: "The government has better places to spend money than devoting resources to a strong conservation program."

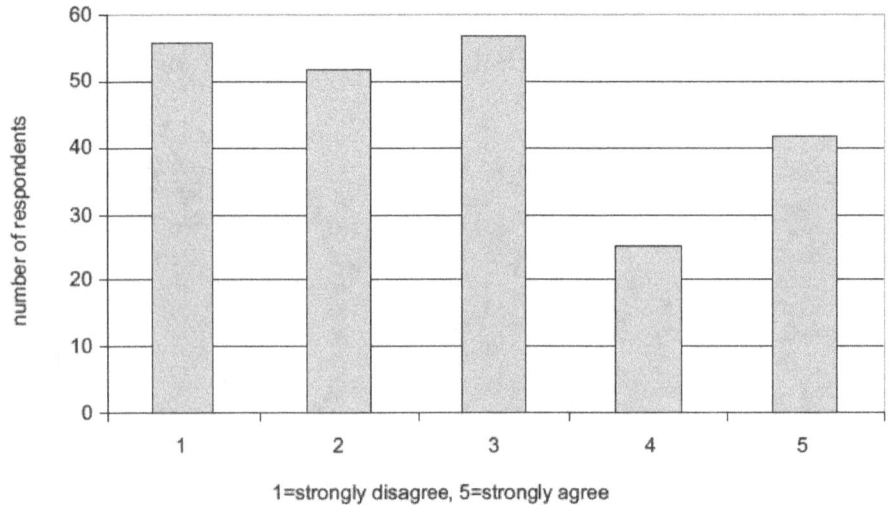

Figure 21—Distribution of responses to: "The most important role for the public lands is providing jobs and income for local people."

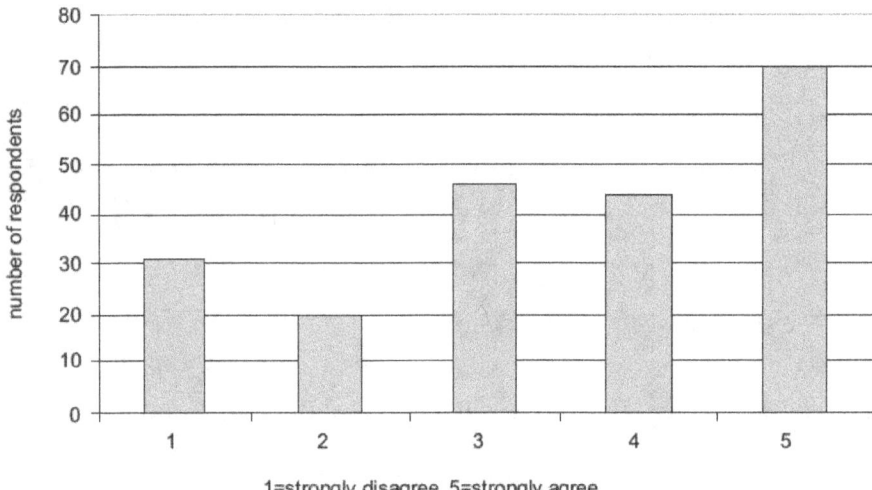

Figure 22—Distribution of responses to: "The main reason for maintaining resources today is so we can use them in the future if we need to."

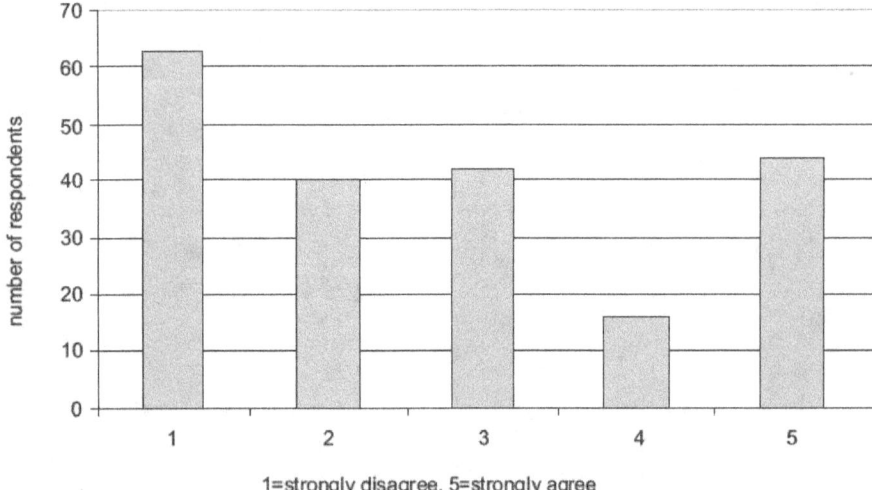

Figure 23—Distribution of responses to: "We should actively harvest more trees to meet the needs of a much larger human population."

Comparison of the Intermountain West with the Rest of the United States

The final section of this report compares the VOBA results for the Intermountain West with the results for the rest of the United States. Tables 8 through 11 present the objectives, beliefs about the role of the agency, and customer satisfaction. These are arranged into the same groups as in the sections above ("Core" Important Objectives, Other Important Objectives, Unimportant Objectives, and Objectives of Moderate Importance). Tables 12 and 13 contain the comparison for the Public Lands

Values. These are arranged into Socially Responsible Individual Values and Socially Responsible Management Values. Discussion focuses on those objectives and values with statistically significant differences.

Objectives Identified as Important

Core Important Objectives

The Intermountain West does not differ significantly from the rest of the United States regarding the importance of any of the "core" objectives (table 8). It does differ, however, in that it believes the role of the USDA Forest Service in implementing the top core objective, "Conserving and protecting forests and grasslands that are the source of our water resources, such as streams, lakes, and watershed areas," is less appropriate than does the rest of the United States (mean for Intermountain

Table 8--Comparison of core important objectives, beliefs, and attitudes between Intermountain West and the rest of the United States.

OBJECTIVE	Is this an important objective for you? *(1=not at all important, 5=very important)*			Do you believe that fulfilling this objective is an appropriate role for the USDA Forest Service? *(1=strongly disagree, 5=strongly agree)*			How favorably do you view the performance of the USDA Forest Service in fulfilling this objective? *(1=very unfavorably, 5=very favorably)*		
	Inter-mountain West	Rest of US	Sig. diff -IW/rest US	Inter-mountain West	Rest of US	Sig. diff -IW/rest US	Inter-mountain West	Rest of US	Sig. diff -IW/ rest US
Conserving and protecting forests and grasslands that are the source of our water resources, such as streams, lakes, and watershed areas.	4.69 *0.78[a]* 110[b]	4.72 *0.75* 1217		4.44 *0.92* 127	4.61 *0.82* 1279	**	3.76 *1.15* 494	3.84 *1.10* 1100	
Developing volunteer programs to improve forests and grasslands (for example, planting trees, or improving water quality).	4.60 *0.76* 107	4.53 *0.88* 1188		4.42 *0.98* 109	4.52 *0.91* 1215		3.41 *1.13* 79	3.75 *1.19* 876	**
Informing the public about recreation concerns on forests and grasslands such as safety, trail etiquette, and respect for wildlife.	4.57 *0.88* 100	4.57 *0.89* 1067		4.44 *0.89* 96	4.52 *0.91* 1058		3.63 *1.21* 106	3.89 *1.17* 1144	**
Allowing for diverse uses of forests and grasslands such as grazing, recreation, and wildlife habitat.	4.21 *0.97* 97	4.04 *1.10* 1033		4.10 *1.08* 78	4.05 *1.13* 881		3.59 *1.07* 76	3.68 *1.08* 773	

[a] Standard deviation
[b] Sample size for each item (n)
*, **, *** mean differences are statistically significant at ∝= 0 05, 0 01, and 0 001 respectively, based on a t-test

West 4.44, for rest of the United States 4.61). However, there is also greater variation in evaluations within the Intermountain West than within the rest of the United States (standard deviation for Intermountain West 0.92, for rest of United States 0.82).

Looking at the other core objectives in table 8, the Intermountain West residents rate agency performance for developing volunteer programs to improve forests and grasslands lower, although still somewhat favorably, than does the rest of the United States (mean for Intermountain West 3.41, mean for rest of United States 3.75). The same is true for informing the public about recreation concerns on forest and grasslands (mean for Intermountain West 3.63, mean for rest of United States 3.89). Although there is substantial disagreement concerning both of these evaluations, the level of disagreement is quite similar between the Intermountain West region and the rest of the United States.

Other Important Objectives

The Intermountain West differs from the rest of the United States in four of the seven other Important Objectives (table 9). Protecting ecosystems and wildlife habitat, informing the public on the potential environmental impacts, and preserving the ability to have a wilderness experience are all less important to residents of the Intermountain West than to residents of other regions. However, there was also less consistency in responses for the Intermountain West residents than for the rest of the United States. The general trends also hold true when looking at appropriateness of the role for the USDA Forest Service and agency performance.

In contrast to the aforementioned objectives, the issue of making local management decisions is more important to the Intermountain West region than to the rest of the United States. People of the Intermountain West also view local management decisions as a more appropriate role for the USDA Forest Service than does the rest of the United States. They reported a less favorable level of agency performance than does the rest of the United States, however.

Objectives Identified as Not Important

Respondents from the Intermountain West differed from the rest of the United States within only one objective: expanding access for motorized off-highway vehicles on forest and grasslands (table 10). Although both respondent groups evaluated the objective as unimportant, the public from the Intermountain West did view it as significantly more important than respondents from the rest of the United States. Consistency of evaluation was nearly the same for both groups.

Moving to appropriateness of the role for the USDA Forest Service, there is no statistically significant difference in the views of the respondents from the Intermountain West and those from the rest of the United States. Finally, the comparison between the Intermountain West public and the rest of the United States revealed only one statistically significant difference in how the two groups view agency performance. The respondents from the Intermountain West evaluated the agency's performance to be less favorable than did the rest of the United States in the development and maintenance of a continuous trail system for motorized vehicles (mean for the Intermountain West, 2.96, for the rest of the United States, 3.22). The standard deviation is nearly the same for both of these groups (s.d. for Intermountain West, 1.17, for the rest of the United States, 1.20).

Objectives Identified as Moderately Important

As was done in the earlier section, results for this group of objectives have been organized in table 11 to facilitate a discussion of related issues. (For example, objectives that deal either directly or indirectly with resource extraction are grouped together.)

Resource extraction and use—The Intermountain West differs from the rest of the United States in rating three of the six objectives of moderate importance that deal with resource extraction and use. All three deal with limiting extractive industries, or the development of extractive industries, such as timber harvesting and mining, in order to preserve forests and grasslands, and in all three the respondents from the Intermountain West considered the objective to be of less importance than did the public from the rest of the United States (table 11). Interestingly, respondents from the rest of the United States considered two of these objectives to be important, and in the third the mean was 3.99, or as close as possible to being an important objective without being placed within that category. Standard deviations were higher than those from the rest of the United States, however, showing less agreement in the Intermountain West.

Similarly, in four of the six objectives, public from the Intermountain West viewed fulfilling the resource extraction and use objectives to be less appropriate roles for the USDA Forest Service than did the rest of the United

Table 9--Comparison of other important objectives, beliefs and attitudes between the Intermountain West and the rest of the United States.

OBJECTIVE	Is this an important objective for you? (1=not at all important, 5=very important)		Sig. diff - IW/rest US	Do you believe that fulfilling this objective is an appropriate role for the USDA Forest Service? (1=strongly disagree, 5=strongly agree)		Sig. diff - IW/rest US	How favorably do you view the performance of the USDA Forest Service in fulfilling this objective? (1=very unfavorably, 5=very favorably)		Sig. diff – IW/rest US
	Inter-mountain West	Rest of US		Inter-mountain West	Rest of US		Inter-mountain West	Rest of US	
Protecting ecosystems and wildlife habitats.	4.32 *1.05* 116	4.57 *0.89* 1406	***	4.34 *1.02* 102	4.58 *0.87* 1220	**	3.59 *1.20* 104	3.88 *1.09* 1154	***
Making management decisions concerning the use of forests and grasslands at the local level rather than at the national level.	4.31 *1.07* 80	3.95 *1.17* 837	***	4.22 *1.08* 73	3.92 *1.22* 1030	**	3.13 *1.50* 68	3.43 *1.23* 737	*
Developing volunteer programs to maintain trails and facilities on forests and grasslands (for example, trail maintenance or campground maintenance).	4.16 *1.07* 93	4.15 *1.04* 1014		4.17 *1.01* 96	4.20 *1.04* 1069		3.61 *1.22* 75	3.73 *1.13* 882	
Informing the public on the economic value received by developing our national resources.	4.01 *1.07* 86	4.02 *1.25* 1026		4.06 *1.16* 77	3.98 *1.21* 994		2.73 *1.33* 80	3.25 *1.28* 906	****
Informing the public on the potential environmental impacts of all uses associated with forests and grasslands.	4.12 *1.08* 82	4.41 *0.98* 1090	**	4.38 *0.95* 92	4.45 *0.93* 1043		3.22 *1.39* 90	3.43 *1.26* 923	
Developing a national policy that guides natural resource development of all kinds (for example, specifies levels of extraction and regulates environmental impacts).	4.16 *1.23* 101	4.23 *1.16* 1194		3.99 *1.18* 90	4.17 *1.15* 1018		3.22 *1.22* 74	3.45 *1.23* 919	
Preserving the ability to have a wilderness experience on forests and grasslands.	4.03 *1.25* 98	4.23 *1.09* 1243	*	3.90 *1.32* 114	4.25 *1.07* 1245	***	3.80 *1.05* 126	3.87 *1.02* 1275	

[a] Standard deviation
[b] Sample size for each item (n)
*, **, *** mean differences are statistically significant at α= 0 05, 0 01, and 0 001 respectively, based on a t-test

Table 10--Comparison of the objectives, beliefs and attitudes identified as not important by Intermountain West with the rest of the United States.

OBJECTIVE	Is this an important objective for you? (1=not at all important, 5=very important)			Do you believe that fulfilling this objective is an appropriate role for the USDA Forest Service? (1=strongly disagree, 5=strongly agree)			How favorably do you view the performance of the USDA Forest Service in fulfilling this objective? (1=very unfavorably, 5=very favorably)		
	Inter-mountain West	Rest of US	Sig. diff IW/rest US	Inter-mountain West	Rest of US	Sig. diff -IW/rest US	Inter-mountain West	Rest of US	Sig. diff –IW/rest US
Developing new paved roads on forests and grasslands for access for cars and recreational vehicles.	2.38 *1.30*[a] *80*[b]	2.39 *1.37* 1030		2.33 *1.35* 92	2.47 *1.41* 1141		3.14 *1.20* 74	3.13 *1.25* 850	
Expanding access for motorized off-highway vehicles on forests and grasslands (for example, snowmobiling or 4-wheel driving).	2.60 *1.55* 92	2.24 *1.38* 1037	**	2.52 *1.40* 100	2.41 *1.37* 1172		2.88 *1.30* 75	2.96 *1.29* 751	
Expanding commercial recreation on forests and grasslands (for example, ski areas, guide services, or outfitters).	2.87 *1.24* 81	2.87 *1.31* 996		2.92 *1.40* 106	3.03 *1.36* 1192		3.38 *1.05* 56	3.36 *1.16* 832	
Making the permitting process easier for some established uses of forests and grasslands such as grazing, logging, mining, and commercial recreation.	2.93 *1.37* 86	2.72 *1.40* 978		2.86 *1.47* 84	2.64 *1.43* 1050		2.87 *1.25* 71	2.97 *1.27* 696	
Developing and maintaining continuous trail systems that cross both public and private land for motorized vehicles such as snowmobiles or ATVs.	2.94 *1.46* 90	2.76 *1.41* 1192		2.86 *1.50* 93	2.80 *1.44* 1030		2.96 *1.17* 78	3.22 *1.20* 859	*

[a] Standard deviation

[b] Sample size for each item (n).

*, **, *** mean differences are statistically significant at α= 0.05, 0.01, and 0.001 respectively, based on a t-test.

States. Finally, the Intermountain West respondents also consistently viewed agency performance surrounding resource extraction and use less favorably than did the rest of the United States. (See the data recorded in table 11.) These differences may reflect the fact that the much of the nation's resource extraction occurs on land within the Intermountain West region.

Public input and information—Of the two objectives of moderate importance that deal with public input and information, one, encouraging collaboration between groups in order to share information concerning uses of

forests and grasslands, is considered to be less important by the public of the Intermountain West (mean for the Intermountain West, 3.98, mean for the rest of the United States, 4.23). As is the case in most of the aforementioned cases, the lower mean is also paired with a higher standard deviation, showing less agreement among the respondents of the Intermountain West than of the rest of the United States (s.d. for the Intermountain West, 1.17, s.d. for the rest of the United States, 1.08). Despite the difference with the importance of the objective, people from the Intermountain West are in agreement with people from the

Table 11--Comparison of the objectives, beliefs and attitudes identified as moderately important by the Intermountain West with the rest of the United States.

OBJECTIVE	Is this an important objective for you? (1=not at all important, 5=very important)		Sig. diff-IW/rest US	Do you believe that fulfilling this objective is an appropriate role for the USDA Forest Service? (1=strongly disagree, 5=strongly agree)		Sig. diff–IW/rest US	How favorably do you view the performance of the USDA Forest Service in fulfilling this objective? (1=very unfavorably, 5=very favorably)		Sig. diff–IW/rest US
	Inter-mountain West	Rest of US		Inter-mountain West	Rest of US		Inter-mountain West	Rest of US	
Resource Extraction and Use Objectives									
Preserving the natural resources of forests and grasslands through such policies as no timber harvesting or no mining.	3.86 *1.34[a]* 111[b]	4.17 *1.21* 1248	**	3.65 *1.52* 110	4.17 *1.22* 1233	****	3.32 *1 28* 97	3.63 *1.22* 1072	**
Preserving the cultural uses of forests and grasslands by Native Americans and Native Hispanics such as firewood gathering, her/berry/plant gathering, and ceremonial access.	3.82 *1.31* 113	3.78 *1.29* 1241		3.43 *1.31* 101	3.67 *1.31* 1362	*	3.38 *0.07* 78	3.40 *1.23* 942	
Designating more wilderness areas on public land that stops access for development and motorized uses.	3.82 *1.28* 109	3.85 *1.28* 966		3.42 *1.60* 91	3.68 *1.39* 1000	*	3.01 *1.37* 80	3.32 *1.23* 821	**
Providing natural resources from forests and grasslands to support communities dependent on grazing, mining, or timber harvesting.	3.69 *1.27* 90	3.54 *1.33* 1016		3.37 *1.19* 83	3.24 *1.37* 993		3.29 *1.15* 94	3.36 *1.17* 950	
Restricting mineral development on forests and grasslands.	3.55 *1.45* 88	4.03 *1.26* 1004	****	3.78 *1.46* 86	3.95 *1.34* 1037		3.04 *1.30* 110	3.33 *1.36* 818	**
Restricting timber harvesting and grazing on forests and grasslands.1	3.54 *1.56* 90	3.99 *1.22* 1052	***	3.36 *1.49* 97	4.00 *1.49* 974	****	3.09 *1.30* 69	3.31 *1.29* 877	
Public Input and Information Objectives									
Encouraging collaboration between groups in order to share information concerning uses of forests and grasslands.	3.98 *1.17* 82	4.23 *1.08* 984	**	4.21 *1.07* 84	4.20 *1.04* 983		3.70 *1.14* 79	3.55 *1.14* 822	
Using public advisory committees to advise on public land management issues.	3.77 *1.17* 70	3.85 *1.16* 900		4.00 *1.15* 74	3.87 *1.15* 853		3.14 *1.09* 59	3.34 *1.19* 661	

[a] Standard deviation
[b] Sample size for each item (n).
*, **, ***, **** mean differences are statistically significant at α=0.10, 0.05, 0.01, and 0.001 respectively, based on a t-test.

rest of the United States when it comes to evaluating the appropriateness of the role for the USDA Forest Service and the performance of the agency for the public input and information objectives. (See table 11.)

Recreation—Within the group of four objectives dealing with recreation, there are no statistically significant differences between the responses of the Intermountain West and those of the rest of the United States. The Intermountain West region does report a lower evaluation of appropriateness, however, for the USDA Forest Service's role in increasing law enforcement efforts by public lands agencies. The Intermountain West respondents also evaluate the agency performance less favorably than does the public from the rest of the United States on two objectives: designating some existing recreation trails for specific use, and paying an entry fee that goes to support public land.

Land acquisition—The final two moderately important objectives, as evaluated by the Intermountain West public, focus on land acquisition issues. One, increasing the total number of acres in the public land system, is evaluated by the Intermountain West public to be significantly less important than it is for public in the rest of the United States (mean for the Intermountain West, 3.39, mean for the rest of the United States, 3.70). However, in the other areas of evaluation—appropriateness of role for the USDA Forest Service and performance of the agency—the respondents from the Intermountain West agree with those from the rest of the United States.

Public Lands Values

Socially Responsible Individual Values

Table 12 compares the Intermountain West respondent's Socially Responsible Individual Values with those of the rest of the United States. The mean for the Intermountain West is at least somewhat lower than for the rest of the United States in all but 1 of the 13 values, statistically lower in 5. Since a higher mean in the value statements indicates a higher level of environmental orientation, this suggests the respondents from the Intermountain West are generally not as environmentally oriented as are respondents in other parts of the United States.

Socially Responsible Management Values

The mean responses of the Socially Responsible Management Values from the Intermountain West are lower in all cases where there is a statistically significant difference (table 13). These values statements are worded so that higher responses indicate greater value

placed on the extraction and use of natural resources. Thus, while respondents from the Intermountain West exhibit a lower level of environmental orientation for the Individual Values, they also exhibit a lower preference for human-centered uses of forests and grasslands when responding to the Management Values. Although there are many possible explanations for this reaction, one possibility may be the general desire within the Intermountain West to minimize government involvement. Following this outlook, and bearing in mind that respondents may interpret many of these values as asking about public lands instead of private lands, people within the Intermountain West may react less favorably to anything they view as increasing government involvement.

Highlights of a Comparison of the Intermountain West with Regions 8 and 9_____

As part of the Chief's Regional Review process, reports similar to this one were prepared for USDA Forest Service Southern Region (8) and Eastern Region (9). The availability of results from these two Regions allows for a general comparison among respondents in the Intermountain West region and those in Region 8 and Region 9. Tables 14 through 18 show these comparisons. Discussion of the comparisons focuses on the core objectives (those with very high means and low standard deviations) and the important objectives (with high means, but also higher standard deviations).

Core Important Objectives

Residents in both Regions and the Intermountain West indicated the preservation of watersheds to be the most important objective. The preservation of watersheds objective also has high degree of consensus within each of the regions. Likewise, all respondents find the development of volunteer programs to improve the land and informing the public about recreation concerns, to also be core objectives. Despite these three similarities, the last core objective for Intermountain West respondents, allowance of diverse uses of forest and grasslands, is only considered to be important, meaning there was a lack of consensus, by Regions 8 and 9. Table 14 lays out the variation among the Regions.

Table 12--Comparison of socially responsible individual values--the Intermountain West and the rest of the United States.

VALUES (1=strongly agree, 5=strongly disagree)	Intermountain West	Rest of US	Significant difference between Intermountain West and the rest of the US
I am glad there are National Forests even if I never get to see them.	4.74 0.74[a] 189[b]	4.75 0.73 1860	
Manufacturers should be encouraged to use recycled materials in their manufacturing and processing operations.	4.63 0.80 156	4.65 0.79 1842	
People should be more concerned about how our public lands are used.	4.46 0.97 164	4.68 0.76 1652	****
Future generations should be as important as the current one in the decisions about public lands.	4.45 0.97 185	4.60 0.84 1921	**
Consumers should be interested in the environmental consequences of the products they purchase.	4.38 0.97 158	4.49 0.89 1694	
Donating time or money to worthy causes is important to me.	4.20 0.97 172	4.19 1.02 1659	
People can think public lands are valuable even if they do not actually go there themselves.	4.48 1.00 180	4.63 0.81 1643	**
I am willing to make personal sacrifices for the sake of slowing down pollution.	4.27 1.01 155	4.37 0.94 1679	
People should urge their friends to limit their use of products made from scarce resources.	4.04 1.21 181	4.14 1.11 1851	
I have often thought that if we could just get by with a little less there would be more left for future generations.	3.94 1.23 157	4.05 1.22 1595	
I am willing to stop buying products from companies that pollute the environment even though it might be inconvenient.	3.86 1.25 169	3.97 1.15 1697	
Forests have a right to exist for their own sake, regardless of human concerns and uses.	3.96 1.29 166	4.12 1.17 1786	*
Natural resource must be preserved even if people must do without some products.	3.83 1.34 191	4.12 1.14 1824	****

[a] Standard deviation

[b] Sample size for each item (n).

*, **, ***, **** mean differences are statistically significant at α=0.10, 0.05, 0.01, and 0.001 respectively, based on a t-test.

Table 13--Comparison of socially responsible management values--the Intermountain West and the rest of the United States.

VALUES (1=strongly agree, 5=strongly disagree)	Inter-mountain West	Rest of US	Significant difference between Intermountain West and the rest of the US
The Federal government should subsidize the development and leasing of public lands to companies.	1.93 *1.20*[a] *207*[b]	2.15 *1.38* *2124*	**
I think that the public land managers are doing an adequate job of protecting natural resources from being overused.	3.03 *1.21* *190*	3.09 *1.18* *1974*	
The decision to develop resources should be based mostly on economic grounds.	2.70 *1.29* *192*	2.70 *1.36* *2093*	
The primary use of forests should be for products that are useful to humans.	2.47 *1.30* *238*	2.70 *1.44* *2309*	**
The government has better places to spend money than devoting resources to a strong conservation program.	2.38 *1.39* *194*	2.24 *1.30* *2156*	
The most important role for the public lands is providing jobs and income for local people.	2.76 *1.40* *232*	2.93 *1.40* *2348*	*
The main reason for maintaining resources today is so we can develop them in the future if we need to.	3.48 *1.41* *211*	3.72 *1.37* *2101*	**
We should actively harvest more trees to meet the needs of a much larger human population.	2.70 *1.51* *205*	2.56 *1.53* *2138*	

[a] Standard deviation

[b] Sample size for each item (n).

*, **, ***, **** mean differences are statistically significant at α=0.10, 0.05, 0.01, and 0.001 respectively, based on a t-test.

Table 14--Comparison (mean, standard deviation, and n) among core important objectives for the Intermountain West region and Forest Service Regions 8 and 9.

OBJECTIVE	Intermountain West	Region 8	Region 9
Conserving and protecting forests and grasslands that are the source of our water resources, such as streams, lakes, and watershed areas.	4.69 *0.78*[a] *110*[b]	4.70 *0.77* *479*	4.76 *0.67* *530*
Developing volunteer programs to improve forests and grasslands (for example, planting trees, or improving water quality).	4.60 *0.76* *107*	4.61 *0.76* *405*	4.53 *0.85* *545*
Informing the public about recreation concerns on forests and grasslands such as safety, trail etiquette, and respect for wildlife.	4.57 *0.88* *100*	4.55 *0.88* *378*	4.52 *0.92* *490*
Allowing for diverse uses of forests and grasslands such as grazing, recreation, and wildlife habitat.	4.21 *0.97* *97*	4.01 *1.21* *385*	4.05 *1.12* *444*

[a] Standard deviation

[b] Sample size for each item (n).

Table 15--Comparison (mean, standard deviation, and n) of important objectives for the Intermountain West region and Forest Service Regions 8 and 9.

OBJECTIVE	Intermountain West	Region 8	Region 9
Protecting ecosystems and wildlife habitats.	4.32 *1.05*[a] 116[b]	4.58 *0.91* 488	4.60 *0.87* 642
Making management decisions concerning the use of forests and grasslands at the local level rather than at the national level.	4.31 *1.07* 80	4.15 *1.12* 303	3.90 *1.19* 370
Developing volunteer programs to maintain trails and facilities on forests and grasslands (for example, trail maintenance, or campground maintenance).	4.16 *1.07* 93	4.20 *1.15* 373	4.13 *1.05* 445
Informing the public on the economic value received by developing our natural resources.	4.01 *1.07* 86	3.95 *1.33* 370	4.08 *1.19* 450
Informing the public on the potential environmental impacts of all uses associated with forests and grasslands.	4.12 *1.08* 82	4.53 *0.84* 412	4.42 *0.99* 499
Developing a national policy that guides natural resource development of all kinds (for example, specifies levels of extraction, and regulates environmental impacts).	4.16 *1.23* 101	4.20 *1.20* 414	4.32 *1.09* 553
Preserving the ability to have a "wilderness" experience on forests and grasslands.	4.03 *1.25* 98	4.08 *1.17* 457	4.29 *1.11* 536

[a] Standard deviation
[b] Sample size for each item (n).

Table 16--Comparison (mean, standard deviation, and n) among objectives the Intermountain West Region does not view as important with Forest Service Regions 8 and 9.

OBJECTIVE	Intermountain West	Region 8	Region 9
Developing new paved roads on forests and grasslands for access for cars and recreational vehicles.	2.38 *1.30*[a] 80[b]	2.66 *1.49* 371	2.36 *1.34* 457
Expanding access for motorized off-highway vehicles on forests and grasslands (for example, snowmobiling or 4-wheel driving).	2.60 *1.55* 92	2.30 *1.37* 368	2.22 *1.41* 469
Expanding commercial recreation on forests and grasslands (for example, ski areas, guide services, outfitters).	2.87 *1.24* 81	3.04 *1.38* 369	2.88 *1.30* 440
Making the permitting process easier for some established uses of forests and grasslands such as grazing, logging, mining, and commercial recreation.	2.93 *1.37* 86	3.13 *1.51* 354	2.60 *1.34* 425
Developing and maintaining continuous trail systems that cross both public and private land for motorized vehicles such as snowmobiles or ATVs.	2.94 *1.46* 90	3.02 *1.37* 426	2.71 *1.45* 512

[a] Standard deviation
[b] Sample size for each item (n).

Table 17--Comparison (mean, standard deviation, and n) among objectives the Intermountain West Region views as moderately important with Forest Service Regions 8 and 9.

OBJECTIVE		Intermountain West	Region 8	Region 9
Resource Extraction and Use	Preserving the natural resources of forests and grasslands through such policies as no timber harvesting or no mining.	3.86 *1.34[a]* 111[b]	4.25 *1.20* 441	4.25 *1.12* 586
	Preserving the cultural uses of forests and grasslands by Native Americans and Native Hispanics such as fire wood gathering, herb/berry/plant gathering, and ceremonial uses.	3.82 *1.31* 113	3.82 *1.29* 442	3.79 *1.27* 554
	Designating more wilderness areas on public land that stops access for development and motorized uses.	3.82 *1.39* 109	3.86 *1.27* 358	3.98 *1.21* 451
	Providing natural resources from forests and grasslands to support communities depending on grazing, mining, or timber harvesting.	3.69 *1.27* 90	3.68 *1.35* 390	3.51 *1.33* 440
	Restricting mineral development on forests and grasslands.	3.55 *1.45* 88	4.12 *1.31* 371	4.07 *1.24* 456
	Restricting timber harvesting and grazing on forests and grasslands.	3.54 *1.56* 90	4.11 *1.11* 360	4.01 *1.20* 478
Public Input & Information	Encouraging collaboration between groups in order to share information concerning uses of forests and grasslands.	3.98 *1.17* 82	4.21 *0.99* 364	4.23 *1.08* 423
	Using public advisory committees to advise on public land management issues.	3.77 *1.17* 70	3.94 *1.16* 304	3.85 *1.14* 409
Recreation	Developing and maintaining continuous trail systems that cross both public and private land for non-motorized recreation such as hiking or cross-country skiing.	3.91 *1.14* 85	3.59 *1.31* 384	3.85 *1.22* 454
	Increasing law enforcement efforts by public land agencies on public lands.	3.76 *1.23* 66	4.11 *1.04* 334	3.83 *1.27* 400
	Designating some existing recreation trails for specific uses (for example, creating separate trails for snowmobiling and cross-country skiing, or for mountain biking and horseback riding).	3.76 *1.29* 85	3.49 *1.46* 370	3.74 *1.24* 489
	Paying an entry fee that goes to support public land.	3.47 *1.34* 77	3.84 *1.28* 307	3.56 *1.29* 400
Land Acquisition	Increasing the total number of acres in the public land system.	3.39 *1.43* 77	3.73 *1.35* 314	3.84 *1.25* 411
	Allowing public land managers to trade public lands for private lands (for example, to eliminate private property within public land boundaries, or to acquire unique areas of land).	3.14 *1.54* 71	2.88 *1.47* 293	3.07 *1.35* 338

[a] Standard deviation

[b] Sample size for each item (n).

Other Important Objectives

Other important objectives consist of those that have high means but lower consensus. The list of important objectives, as evaluated by the Intermountain West, differs from both Regions 8 and 9 in three objectives. The Intermountain West respondents' evaluations were less consistent on two objectives than the evaluations of the other groups. Both protecting ecosystems and wildlife habitats and informing the public on potential environmental impacts are classified as core objectives for Regions 8 and 9, while respondents from the Intermountain West classified both of these objectives as important. This variation reveals that, although all groups see these objectives as important, there is lower consensus for this evaluation within the Intermountain West.

In contrast, there are also two objectives that were evaluated as more important by the Intermountain West than by other groups. The objective dealing with local management decision making is viewed as important in the Intermountain West, yet is considered to be only moderately important by Region 9. Respondents from Region 8 agreed with the Intermountain West and evaluated the objective as important. Finally, as revealed in table 15, the Intermountain West and Region 9 agree that the objective concerning informing the public on economic values is an important objective, while Region 8 views informing on economics as only moderately important.

Objectives Identified as Not Important

Respondents from the Intermountain West and Region 9 identified the same objectives as not important. Region 8 showed greater variation than the other groups in evaluating objectives viewed as not important. Table 16 displays the variation.

Objectives Identified as Moderately Important

The final category of moderately important objectives shows some variation among the Regions. As table 17 displays, the vast majority of the variation is between evaluations of important and moderately important. Overall comparisons reveal that the Intermountain West differs most from Region 8 (the southern United States).

Concluding Remarks

Data extracted from the VOBA survey reveals the Intermountain West public's objectives for the management of forests and rangelands, beliefs about whether it is the role of the Forest Service to fulfill these objectives, and attitudes about the performance of the agency in fulfilling the objectives. Additionally, these data show this public's environmental values as they relate to public lands.

The most important objective to these respondents was a concern for conserving and protecting forest and grasslands that are the source of water resources. This is not surprising from a region with limited water supplies. Objectives not viewed as important within the Intermountain West region mainly deal with development of access for motorized vehicles (on and off road), although the evaluation of these objectives also has the least consensus.

Finally, the report also compared the responses from the Intermountain West to those in the rest of the United States, and then to two Forest Service Regions. Overall results from the Intermountain West are quite similar to those of the United States as a whole. The results do show a stronger tendency towards allowing access for diverse uses, however, and slightly less of a trend toward protection of ecosystems than do the other Regions and the rest of the United States.

Appendix

Survey Design and Implementation

Between September 1999 and June 2000 over 80 focus groups and individual interviews were conducted across the lower 48 States. These efforts concentrated on three topics: 1) issues related to the use of public lands in general and forests and rangelands in particular, 2) the objectives (or goals) of the group (or individual) regarding the use, management, and conservation of the forests and rangelands, and 3) the role of the Forest Service in the use, management and conservation of the forests and rangelands.

Based upon the results of the focus group interviews, an objectives hierarchy was constructed for each group. These hierarchies indicated what each group or individual was attempting to achieve, and how they would achieve each goal or objective. These objectives ranged from the abstract strategic level to the more specific or applied means level. The means level objectives are at the bottom of the hierarchy, while the strategic objective is at the top. Fundamental objectives between the means level and the strategic level completed the hierarchies. Therefore, the strategic level objective is an abstract objective that can be achieved by more specific fundamental level objectives, which are in turn achieved by means-level objectives (figure 1).

Each of the objectives hierarchies was confirmed with its respective group so as to ensure that it accurately reflected the group's goals and objectives. A combined objectives hierarchy was then constructed that included all the objectives stated by each group or individual interviewed. The result was a hierarchy that covered five strategic level objectives related to access, preservation/conservation, commodity development, education, and natural resource management. These 5 strategic level objectives were supported by 30 fundamental objectives.

The 30 fundamental level objectives were used to develop 30 objectives statements that were utilized in the National Survey of Recreation and the Environment (NSRE). The NSRE is a national survey administered via telephone interviews. The 30 objectives statements were divided into 5 groups based upon the strategic level objectives the focus groups had identified. During the telephone interviews, each respondent was asked one statement from each of the five strategic level groups in order to obtain a statistically valid sample for each statement and for each strategic level group.

As noted above, the survey of the American public's values, objectives, beliefs and attitudes (hereafter VOBA) was conducted as a module within the NSRE. Although questions about respondents' recreation behavior comprise the bulk of the interview, the results presented here are based solely on the questions in the VOBA Module of the survey and the demographic questions. The VOBA questions are sets of scale items to which people are asked to respond using a 5-point scale. The objectives items are anchored by 1=not at all important to 5=very important. Beliefs are anchored by 1=strongly disagree to 5=strongly agree and attitudes are anchored by 1=very unfavorable to 5=very favorable. Each of these 3 scales consists of 30 items. The 25 items in the "values" scale are anchored by 1=strongly disagree and 5=strongly agree.

Reverse Scoring

When the VOBA was designed, care was taken to avoid the appearance of an instrument biased toward or against a specific position. To do this the "direction" of the scale varied. For example, for one item a "strongly agree" response might indicate a conservation/preservation orientation, while for another item the same response might indicate a development orientation. While this is useful to increase the acceptance of the instrument and subsequent response rates, it creates problems when items with the opposite direction are grouped.

To compare two or more items that have opposite directions, it is necessary to make all the items move in the same direction. For example, suppose we want to examine the overall preference for sweets as indicated by the preference for ice cream and pie. We have two scale items. For each, 1 indicates "strongly disagree" and 5 indicates "strongly agree" as in the Public Lands Values scale. To avoid the appearance of bias toward or against sweets, the two items move in opposite directions: "I like ice cream" and "I don't like pie." Clearly a person who likes all sweets will answer 5 to the first item and 1 to the second. Conversely, someone who does not like sweets will answer 1 to the first and 5 to the second. If these items are grouped, it would be more useful for research if both items are scored in the same direction to indicate preference for sweets (either with a higher or lower response for both items). To achieve this, to re-score, we choose one of the items, in this example we'll choose the second, and reverse the scoring. An answer of 5 thus becomes a 1, an answer of 4 becomes 2, 3 remains the same (neutral), 2 becomes 4, and 1 becomes 5. This in effect creates a new item (which could be reworded as "I like pie") that corresponds in direction to "I like ice cream." This re-scoring allows the researcher an overall, consistent indication of each respondent's preference for sweets. Higher numbers for each item indicate a higher preference for sweets, lower numbers indicate lower preference. A similar re-scoring was done for certain items in the VOBA to more accurately characterize overall preferences for item groups.